Homemade healthy dog food cookbook:

2 in 1 guide and cookbook with Simple, Fast, Nutritious, and Scrumptious Recipes. A balanced vet-approved diet to boost your pet's longevity and happiness.

By Spike Fleming

Copyright © 2024 by Spike Fleming

All rights reserved. No part of this publication may be reproduced, distributed, or transmitted in any form or by any means, including photocopying, recording, or other electronic or mechanical methods, without the prior written permission of the author, except in the case of brief quotations embodied in critical reviews and specific other noncommercial uses permitted by copyright law.

Legal notice:

This book, titled "HOMEMADE HEALTHY DOG FOOD COOKBOOK," is authored by Spike Fleming and is fully protected under copyright laws. Any unauthorized distribution, reproduction, or use of the book, in whole or part, is prohibited and may result in legal actions against you. Any use of this book without the author's or the publisher's permission is a violation of their legal rights.

Disclaimer notice:

The content in " HOMEMADE HEALTHY DOG FOOD COOKBOOK " is intended solely for informational and educational purposes. The recipes and guidance in this book are not meant to substitute for professional medical advice or treatment. Readers are strongly advised to consult with a professional before adopting any dietary or health changes for your dog, especially those with pre-existing health conditions. The author, Spike Fleming, has ensured the accuracy of the information presented in this cookbook; however, they do not assume liability for any errors, omissions, or differing interpretations of the content. Neither the publisher nor Spike Fleming shall be held liable for any direct or indirect damages resulting from the use of this book. The reader assumes all responsibility for using the information in this book. The author and the publisher reserve the right to make changes to this book's content without notice.

Table of Contents

Introduction 1

Part 1: The Ultimate Guide 2

Chapter 1: Canine Nutrition Basics 2
Why consider homemade food? 3
Most nutritious foods 4
Foods to Avoid 5

Chapter 2: Transitioning 7
Initial Steps for Transitioning 7
Monitoring health 7
Tackling Common Transition Challenges 9

Chapter 3: Designing meals tailored to your dog's diet 11
Adapting Recipes by Dog Size and Age 11
Catering to Picky Eaters 14
Food allergies 14
Cooking for Dogs with Specific Health Conditions 15

Chapter 4: Life Stage Recipes 17
.... 17
Puppy Recipes 17
    Breakfast Porridge 17
    Chicken and Rice Dinner 17
    Meatball Treats 18
    Fish Stew 18
Adult Recipes 19
    Beef and Vegetable Casserole 19
    Chicken and Sweet Potato Stew 19
    Salmon and Pea Risotto 20
    Turkey and Pumpkin Treats 20
Senior Recipes 21
    Gentle Chicken and Oatmeal Dinner 21
    Fish and Potato Soft Stew 21
    Turkey Loaf 22
    Soft Beef and Rice Meal 22

Chapter 5: Mastering Meal Prep for Dogs 23
Structuring Meals 23
Kitchen tools for a canine-friendly kitchen 23
Cooking methods 25
Meal prepping tips 27
Storage 28
Mistakes to avoid 29
    10 Secret Ingredients for Shiny Coat and Fresh Breath 32

Part 2: Scrumptious Recipes 34
Treats and rewards 34

- Carrot and Apple Treats 34
- Spinach, Carrot, and Zucchini Treats 35
- Sweet Potato Chewies 35
- Peanut Butter and Pumpkin Dog Treats 36
- Chicken and Rice Dog Biscuits 36
- Sweet Potato Fries for Dogs 37
- Beef and Veggie Balls 37
- Frozen Yogurt Pops 38
- Turkey and Sweet Potato Meatballs 38
- Apple Cinnamon Cookies 39
- Salmon and Sweet Pea Treats 39
- Beefy Squash Bites 40
- Cheesy Veggie Muffins 40
- Apple and Oatmeal Dog Snacks 41
- Chicken and Parsley Bites 41

Soups and broth 42
- Chicken and Pumpkin Broth 42
- Beef and Sweet Potato Soup 42
- Turkey and Rice Comfort Soup 43
- Fish and Parsley Stew 43
- Veggie Broth Delight 44
- Chicken and Barley Broth 44
- Beefy Veggie Soup 45
- Lamb and Mint Soup 45
- Quinoa Vegetable Stew 46
- Duck and Pear Puree 46

Seafood recipes 47
- Salmon and Sweet Potato Jerky 47
- Tuna and Parsley Biscuits 47
- Shrimp and Rice Balls 48
- Cod and Pea Patties 48
- Fish and Pumpkin Crackers 49
- Sardine and Carrot Cookies 49
- Tuna and Sweet Potato Cubes 50
- Herring and Pea Pâté 50
- Salmon and Sweet Potato Dinner 51
- Salmon and Pea Dinner 51

Vegetarian recipes 52
- Quinoa Veggie Patties 52
- Sweet Potato and Lentil Loaf 52
- Vegan Doggy Cookies 53
- Pumpkin and Rice Balls 53
- Broccoli and Chickpea Mash 54
- Green Veggie and Brown Rice Casserole 54

Nutrient-rich recipes 55
- Chicken and Vegetable Flaxseed Dinner 55
- Balanced Beef Stew 56
- Chicken and Rice Dinner 56
- Omega-3 Fish Feast 57
- Turkey and Vegetable Mash 57
- Veggie-Packed Canine Kibble 58
- Protein Power Pupsicles 58
- Hearty Barley and Mushroom Stew 59

- Green Bean Crunchies 59
- Butternut Squash and Lentil Loaf 60
- Beef and Quinoa Dinner 60

Seasonal recipes 61
- Springtime Chicken and Asparagus Meal 61
- Summertime Beef and Zucchini Skewers 61
- Autumn Pumpkin and Turkey Stew 62
- Winter Warm-Up Sweet Potato and Lentil Soup 62
- Cool Cucumber and Yogurt Salad for Summer 63
- Spring Pea and Carrot Rice Bowl 63
- Summer Berry Chicken Salad 64
- Autumn Pumpkin Beef Mash 64
- Winter Warm Barley and Veggie Porridge 65
- Spring Herb Chicken Bake 65

Sophisticated or Deluxe Options 66
- Lobster and Sweet Pea Risotto 66
- Quail Egg and Spinach Omelette 66
- Seared Duck with Blueberry Compote 67
- Gourmet Turkey and Cranberry Dog Feast 67
- Salmon and Dill Delicacy 68
- Beef and Blueberry Bliss 68

Sensitive Stomach Options 69
- Gentle Chicken and Rice 69
- Sensitive Stomach Fish Patties 69
- Turkey and Sweet Potato Mash 70
- Digestive Soothing Oatmeal 70
- Gentle Digest Lamb and Parsnip Puree 71
- Soothing Chicken Broth Bowl 71
- Hypoallergenic Fish Flakes 72
- Fish and Sweet Potato Digestive Health Meal 72

Special Diet Options 73
- Low-Fat Chicken and Vegetable Stew for Weight Management 73
- Hypoallergenic Fish and Sweet Potato Mash for Allergies 73
- High-Fiber Beef and Pumpkin Recipe for Digestive Health 74
- Kidney Care Recipe with Low Phosphorus 74
- Low-Sodium Chicken Soup for Heart Health 75
- Grain-Free Turkey and Vegetable Patties for Dogs with Grain Allergies ... 75
- Antioxidant-Rich Blueberry and Spinach Puree for Immune Support 76
- Omega-3 Rich Salmon and Quinoa Dinner for Skin and Coat Health 76

Fresh, Uncooked Foods 77
- Basic Raw Beef Dinner 77
- Chicken and Apple Raw Meal 77
- Turkey and Cranberry Festive Mix 78
- Salmon and Veggie Raw Blend 78
- Raw Lamb and Mint Mix 79
- Beefy Blueberry Blend 79
- Raw Turkey and Cranberry Delight 80
- Fish and Veggie Raw Feast 80

Part 3: 30-Day Meal Plan 81
Meal Plan for Your Dog 81

Conclusion 83

INTRODUCTION

Welcome to a journey where love for our furry friends meets the kitchen—welcome to your new adventure with "Homemade Healthy Dog Food Cookbook." Ever worried about the unknown additives in your dog's commercial food or noticed your dog's coat losing its luster? Perhaps you've encountered the dreaded bad breath during cuddle times? If these sound familiar, you're not alone, and this book is here to transform those worries into a wholesome, healthful eating routine for your beloved pet.

Crafted by an author with over two decades of experience in dog nutrition and a loving owner to three of the cutest dogs you can imagine, this book is a treasure trove of knowledge and love for dogs of all breeds and sizes. The recipes and tips within these pages stem from years of hands-on experience and learning, aimed at solving the exact problems you face with commercial dog foods.

Imagine a 30-day meal plan specifically designed to ease your dog into a homemade diet, ensuring a balanced, nutritious transition from store-bought foods. This guide includes a secret formula for determining the perfect portion sizes for your pet, considering factors like age, weight, and activity level—taking the guesswork out of mealtime.

Moreover, this cookbook reveals 10 secret ingredients guaranteed to bring back the shine to your dog's coat and freshen their breath. These aren't just any ingredients; they're the result of meticulous research and testing, blended in just the right amounts to promote health and vitality.

The author's expertise doesn't stop at crafting meals. With a background in animal nutrition, our author understands that each dog is unique, requiring tailored dietary plans. This book addresses this with variations in each recipe to suit different dietary needs and preferences

This book does more than just list recipes; it educates you on WHY each ingredient benefits your dog and HOW you can continue to adapt and create recipes on your own. It empowers you to make informed decisions about your dog's health, offering peace of mind that each meal is packed with nutrition.

Begin this exciting new chapter in your dog care journey as we delve into the basics of homemade dog nutrition in the first chapter. Here, you'll lay the groundwork for a healthier, happier life for your beloved companion. Let's get started!

Part 1: The Ultimate Guide

CHAPTER 1: CANINE NUTRITION BASICS

Welcome to the exciting world of homemade dog food, where every ingredient you choose plays a vital role in your furry companion's health and happiness. This guide isn't just about mixing meats and veggies; it's about understanding the science of canine nutrition and using it to enrich your dog's life. Let's dive into the key components of canine nutrition, sprinkled with facts and stats that highlight their importance, making your journey into homemade dog food not only informative but also engaging.

The Power of Protein

Did you know that dogs can require up to twice the amount of protein humans do, relative to their size? Protein is the cornerstone of a healthy dog diet, crucial for muscle repair, skin health, and hair growth. The right protein can make your dog's coat glossier than a magazine cover and keep their muscles as strong as a mini superhero. Aim for high-quality sources like chicken, beef, and fish to keep your dog in peak condition.

The Energy Boosters: Fats and Carbohydrates

Fats are not foes; they're your dog's best fuel. They deliver a potent energy punch—more than double the energy of proteins or carbohydrates. Omega-3 and omega-6 fatty acids, found in salmon and flaxseed, aren't just buzzwords; they're the secret to a shiny coat and healthy skin. But balance is key. An excess can lead to weight issues, considering that approximately 56% of dogs in the U.S. are overweight or obese, according to the Association for Pet Obesity Prevention.

Carbohydrates, often viewed with skepticism, actually play a critical role in providing energy and supporting a healthy digestive system. They're the dietary equivalent of a marathon runner's pasta dinner. However, choosing the right carbs is crucial. Whole grains and vegetables provide not only energy but also essential fiber, vitamins, and minerals.

The Unsung Heroes: Vitamins and Minerals

Vitamins and minerals might not get the spotlight in your dog's diet, but they're the behind-the-scenes crew that keeps the show running. Each vitamin and mineral has a specific role, from supporting bone health to bolstering the immune system. For instance, calcium isn't just for strong bones; it's also vital for nerve function and blood clotting. A varied diet ensures your dog gets this dynamic team of nutrients they need to thrive.

Water: The Essence of Life

Perhaps the most crucial yet overlooked nutrient is water. A dog can lose all its fat and half its protein and survive, but a mere 10% loss of body water can cause serious illness. Always ensure your dog has access to fresh, clean water to keep them hydrated and healthy.

The Balance is in the Bowl

Creating the perfect bowl of homemade dog food is about finding the right balance. It's not just a meal; it's a mosaic of nutrients, each piece essential to the overall picture of health. Remember, what works for one dog might not suit another. Factors like age, activity level, and health conditions mean that nutrition is not one-size-fits-all.

The Homemade Promise

Crafting homemade meals for your dog is a promise—a promise of health, happiness, and a deepened bond. Each meal is an opportunity to show love, to choose ingredients that cater to your dog's unique needs and preferences. It's about embracing the science of nutrition and translating it into a bowlful of love. Let's make every meal a step towards a healthier, happier dog. Welcome to the homemade revolution, where every ingredient counts, and every meal matters.

Why consider homemade food?

The decision to switch to homemade dog food is more than just a dietary change; it's a commitment to enhancing your dog's life with every bite. Let's explore the compelling reasons to embrace homemade meals, armed with examples, facts, and the pure joy of crafting dishes that wag tails and warm hearts.

Imagine a world where every meal is tailored to your specific nutritional needs, tastes, and preferences. This isn't a luxury reserved for humans alone; it's the essence of homemade dog food. Unlike commercial options, which strive for a one-size-fits-all solution, homemade meals can be customized to address your dog's unique requirements, including allergies, sensitivities, and health conditions.

According to a study by the Cummings School of Veterinary Medicine at Tufts University, more than half of the commercial pet foods studied did not meet standard nutritional guidelines. This highlights the challenge of finding a commercial food that truly fits your dog's needs.

The journey from farm to bowl is often a mystery with commercial dog food. In contrast, homemade meals are crafted from fresh, whole ingredients that you select yourself. This control over the quality and source of ingredients means less processing, fewer preservatives, and no hidden fillers—just pure, unadulterated goodness.

A homemade meal could include freshly cooked salmon, rich in omega-3 fatty acids for shiny coats, alongside vibrant green beans and sweet potatoes, packed with fiber and vitamins. Compare this to a commercial dry food label with unpronounceable ingredients, and the choice becomes clear.

Preparing meals for your dog is an act of love, a daily ritual that strengthens the bond between you. It's about more than just nutrition; it's a way to connect with your dog, understanding their likes and dislikes, and seeing the joy in their eyes as they dig into a meal made just for them.

A survey conducted by the American Pet Products Association revealed that 95% of pet owners consider their pets to be part of the family. What better way to show family love than through carefully prepared, nutritious meals?

While the initial thought might be that homemade dog food is more expensive, it can actually be cost-effective in the long run. By purchasing ingredients in bulk, using seasonal produce, and avoiding the premium prices of high-end commercial foods, you can manage your budget more efficiently.

The cost of high-quality commercial dog food can range from $2 to $5 per pound. In contrast, the average cost of homemade dog food ingredients can be significantly lower, especially if you shop smart and in bulk.

The shift to homemade food often comes with noticeable health benefits. Owners report improvements in their dogs' energy levels, coat quality, weight management, and overall vitality. Moreover, the risk of obesity, diabetes, and other diet-related diseases can decrease with a well-balanced, homemade diet.

Choosing to prepare homemade dog food is a testament to the love and care you have for your canine companion. It's about taking an active role in their health and happiness, understanding their nutritional needs, and enjoying the process of cooking for them. As you embark on this wholesome journey, remember that every scoop, every ingredient, and every meal is a step towards a healthier, happier dog.

Most nutritious foods

In the realm of homemade dog food, certain ingredients stand out as nutritional powerhouses, each bringing a unique set of benefits to your dog's bowl. This chapter delves into the most nutritious foods you can incorporate into your homemade dog meals, turning each feeding time into an opportunity for health and vitality. Let's explore these canine superfoods, their benefits, and how they can be included in your dog's diet.

Lean Proteins: The Muscle Builders

Proteins are the building blocks of your dog's body, essential for muscle growth and repair. Lean meats such as chicken, turkey, beef, and fish offer high-quality protein along with vital nutrients like iron, zinc, and B vitamins.

- **Chicken and Turkey:** Low in fat and high in protein, perfect for maintaining lean muscle mass.
- **Beef:** Rich in iron and zinc, supporting a healthy immune system.
- **Fish:** Salmon and sardines are excellent sources of omega-3 fatty acids, promoting a shiny coat and healthy skin.

Whole Grains: The Energy Sustainers

Whole grains provide dogs with a healthy source of carbohydrates, essential for energy. They also offer fiber, which aids in digestion, along with essential minerals and vitamins.

- **Brown Rice:** Easy to digest and good for energy.
- **Oats:** Rich in fiber, helping to regulate blood glucose levels and bowel movements.
- **Barley:** Contains beta-glucan, a type of soluble fiber that improves digestion and helps control cholesterol.

Vegetables: The Vitamin and Mineral Treasures

Vegetables are a rich source of vitamins, minerals, and fiber, which are crucial for your dog's overall health. They support everything from vision to digestion to immune function.

- **Carrots:** Packed with beta-carotene for eye health and a crunchy treat for dental health.
- **Green Beans:** Low in calories and high in fiber, perfect for weight management.
- **Pumpkin:** High in fiber and beta-carotene, supporting digestive health and vision.

Fruits: The Natural Sweet Treats

Fruits can be a healthy, sweet treat for dogs, offering vitamins, minerals, and antioxidants with a burst of natural sweetness.

- **Apples:** A good source of vitamins A and C, as well as fiber for digestive health. Remember to remove the seeds and core.
- **Blueberries:** Packed with antioxidants, supporting immune health and aging.
- **Bananas:** Rich in potassium and fiber, great for heart and digestive health.

Fats and Oils: The Essential Fatty Acids

The right fats are crucial for your dog's diet, providing energy and supporting cell function, as well as promoting healthy skin and a glossy coat.

- **Flaxseed Oil:** A plant-based source of omega-3 fatty acids, great for skin and coat health.
- **Fish Oil:** Provides EPA and DHA, types of omega-3 fatty acids that support cognitive function and reduce inflammation.
- **Coconut Oil:** Contains medium-chain fatty acids that can help with digestion, coat health, and immune response.

Incorporating these superfoods into your dog's homemade meals is not just about adding them randomly. It's about creating balanced meals that cater to your dog's specific nutritional needs. Here are a few tips:

Start Slow: Introduce new foods gradually to avoid digestive upset.
Balance is Key: Ensure meals are well-balanced with proteins, carbohydrates, and fats.
Consult a Professional: Always consult with a vet or a canine nutritionist to ensure the meals you're preparing meet your dog's dietary needs.

Embracing these nutritious foods in your dog's diet can lead to noticeable improvements in their health, energy, and overall well-being. As you craft meals with these superfoods, remember that each ingredient you choose is an act of love, contributing to your dog's happiness and longevity. Welcome to the delightful world of canine culinary arts, where every meal is a celebration of health and flavor.

Foods to Avoid

In the culinary adventure of homemade dog food, knowledge of what not to feed your furry companion is just as crucial as knowing the right ingredients. While many foods can provide immense health benefits, others pose significant risks to your dog's well-being. This chapter is dedicated to those foods that should never find their way into your dog's bowl, ensuring that your homemade meals are not only nutritious but also safe.

Certain foods are well-known for their toxicity to dogs and must be avoided at all costs to prevent potential health hazards.

- **Chocolate:** Contains theobromine and caffeine, which can be toxic to dogs, leading to vomiting, diarrhea, rapid heartbeat, and even death.
- **Grapes and Raisins:** Can cause kidney failure in dogs. Even a small amount can make a dog ill.
- **Onions and Garlic:** Can destroy a dog's red blood cells, leading to anemia. This includes all forms, raw, cooked, or powder.
- **Xylitol:** A sweetener found in many products, including sugar-free gum and peanut butter. It can cause insulin release, leading to liver failure.

Some foods might seem harmless but can pose hidden dangers to dogs due to their specific components or the way they're prepared.

- **Avocado:** Contains persin, which can cause vomiting and diarrhea in dogs.
- **Macadamia Nuts:** Can cause weakness, depression, vomiting, tremors, and hyperthermia.
- **Raw Meat and Eggs:** Can contain bacteria like Salmonella and E. coli, which are harmful to dogs and humans alike. Raw eggs also have an enzyme that can lead to skin and coat problems.

Fatty Foes: High-Fat Foods

While fats are an essential part of a dog's diet, excessive fat can lead to pancreatitis, a serious and painful condition.

- **Cooked Bones:** Can splinter and cause obstruction or laceration of the digestive system.
- **High-Fat Meats:** Foods rich in saturated fats can lead to obesity and pancreatitis.
- **Butter and Oils:** Excessive amounts can cause upset stomach, diarrhea, and pancreatitis.

Other Foods to Monitor

Certain foods may not be toxic but should be given in moderation or with caution due to potential risks or nutritional imbalances.

- **Dairy Products:** Many dogs are lactose intolerant, and too much dairy can lead to digestive issues.
- **Salty Snacks:** Excessive salt intake can lead to sodium ion poisoning.
- **Corn on the Cob:** The cob can cause intestinal blockage, a serious and potentially fatal condition.

CHAPTER 2: TRANSITIONING

Congratulations! You're ready to embark on a transformative journey with your furry best friend, transitioning from commercial dog food to nutritious, homemade meals. This chapter is your guide through this exciting transition, offering steps, facts, and a sprinkle of fun to ensure a smooth and enjoyable experience for both you and your dog.

Initial Steps for Transitioning

Consultation Is Key Start by talking to your vet. This step is essential to tailor your approach to your dog's specific health requirements, considering their age, breed, and any special needs. It ensures the diet you plan is as beneficial as it is delightful.

Dive Into Dog Nutrition Arm yourself with knowledge about canine nutrition. Understanding what makes a balanced meal—from proteins and carbs to fats and vitamins—is crucial. Also, learn which foods are canine-friendly and which ones are off-limits. This knowledge is your best tool in crafting meals that are safe, nutritious, and irresistible to your pet.

Keep It Simple at First Begin with straightforward recipes that use a few familiar ingredients. This simplicity helps you spot how your dog reacts to each new item, making it easier to identify anything that doesn't agree with them.

Ease Into It Transition slowly by integrating homemade dishes incrementally. Start by mixing a bit of your new creations with their usual fare, gradually upping the homemade content. This gradual shift helps your dog's digestive system adjust without distress.

Watch and Learn As you introduce new meals, keep a keen eye on your dog. How do they react to their new diet? Any changes in energy, digestion, or coat condition? This feedback loop is invaluable, letting you tweak the menu to perfectly suit your pal's palate and health.

Variety Is the Spice of Life Once your dog is comfortable with their new diet, begin to introduce a wider array of ingredients. Mixing up the menu not only keeps your dog interested but also ensures a balanced intake of nutrients. Think of it as crafting a colorful, culinary quilt that keeps your dog healthy and eager for mealtime.

Consistency Counts Regular meal times, consistent portion sizes, and a steady introduction of new dishes help maintain dietary balance and reduce stress for your pet. Consistency means stability, which is vital for your dog's long-term health and happiness.

By following these thoughtful steps, you're not just feeding your dog; you're loving them with every bite they take. This journey of dietary transformation can significantly enhance your dog's vitality and joy, forging an even deeper bond between you as you share in the delights of a healthy, homemade menu.

Monitoring health

Your dog cannot speak in words, but they communicate through their behavior, appearance, and habits. Paying close attention to these details can reveal much about their health and how they're responding to their new diet.

Weight: Keep a weekly log of your dog's weight. A sudden drop or gain can be a tell-tale sign of a dietary imbalance or health issue.

Energy Levels: Note any changes in energy. A healthy diet should maintain or improve your dog's vigor.

Coat and Skin: Look for changes in the coat and skin. A glossy coat and smooth skin are indicators of good nutrition.

There are several checkpoints to consider when monitoring your dog's health through their diet:

Digestive Health

Stool Quality: The condition of your dog's stool is a direct reflection of digestive health. It should be firm and well-formed.

Appetite: A consistent appetite is often a sign of good health, while changes may indicate a dietary issue or health problem.

Physical Health

Body Condition Score: Regularly assess your dog's body condition score. This is a scale used by vets to determine if a pet is underweight, overweight, or at an ideal body weight.

Vitality: A nutritious diet should support overall vitality. A lack of it could suggest nutritional deficiencies.

Behavioral Health

Mood: Observe your dog's mood. Nutrition can influence behavior, and mood changes might signal a reaction to their new diet.

Activity: Monitor your dog's willingness to engage in play and exercise. This can indicate how well their nutritional needs are being met.

Tools for monitoring to help you keep track of your dog's health:

- **Health Journal:** Keep a detailed journal of your dog's daily meals, treats, exercise, behavior, and any health changes.
- **Regular Vet Check-Ups:** Schedule regular vet visits to discuss your observations and make any necessary adjustments to your dog's diet.
- **Nutrition Apps:** Consider using a dog nutrition app to track your dog's food intake and compare it with their nutritional needs.

Engage with a community of like-minded pet parents. Share tips, observe what's working for others, and learn about the vast array of experiences that can guide your own journey. Participate in discussions about homemade dog food and health monitoring on online forums. Attend pet nutrition workshops and seminars to broaden your knowledge and understanding of canine nutrition.

Monitoring your dog's health as you transition to homemade food is a continuous and dynamic process. It's an intimate part of the care you provide, giving you insights into the profound effects of nutrition on their well-being. With each meal, you're not just filling a bowl; you're nurturing a life. So, keep a close watch, enjoy the process, and cherish the wagging tail that greets you at every meal.

Tackling Common Transition Challenges

Challenge 1: Digestive Upsets

One of the first challenges you might face is digestive upset. Signs include changes in stool consistency, gassiness, or occasional vomiting.

Navigating the Solution:

Go Slow: Introduce new foods gradually. Start with a mixture of 75% old food and 25% new, and slowly change the proportions over several days.

Pumpkin Puree: A small amount of canned pumpkin (not pumpkin pie filling) can aid in digestion due to its fiber content.

Challenge 2: Picky Eaters

Some dogs might turn up their noses at new foods, especially if they've been accustomed to one type of food for a long time.

Navigating the Solution:

Mix It Up: Combine homemade food with a bit of their favorite commercial food to make it more appealing.

Warm It Up: Gently warming the food can release aromas and make it more enticing to your dog.

Challenge 3: Balancing the Diet

Creating a balanced homemade diet requires attention to detail. You might worry about including the right amounts of nutrients.

Navigating the Solution:

Consult a Vet: Work with a veterinarian or a pet nutritionist to create balanced meal plans.

High-Quality Supplements: Use vet-recommended supplements to fill any nutritional gaps.

Challenge 4: Time Management

Preparing homemade meals can be time-consuming, which might be challenging for busy pet parents.

Navigating the Solution:

Batch Cooking: Prepare meals in bulk and freeze them in portion-sized containers for easy use.

Crockpot Meals: Use a slow cooker to make dog-friendly stews that can cook throughout the day without much supervision.

Challenge 5: Dealing with Allergies

Transitioning to a new diet may uncover previously unnoticed food sensitivities or allergies in your dog.

Navigating the Solution:

Elimination Diet: If you suspect an allergy, work with your vet to implement an elimination diet to identify the culprit.

Hypoallergenic Options: Choose novel proteins and hypoallergenic ingredients to reduce the risk of allergic reactions.

Challenge 6: Weight Fluctuations

Your dog might gain or lose weight unexpectedly as their body adjusts to the homemade diet.

Navigating the Solution:

Regular Weigh-Ins: Keep a weekly log of your dog's weight to monitor any significant changes.

Adjust Portions: Tailor meal sizes according to your dog's activity level and weight management needs.

Challenge 7: Ensuring Variety

Just like humans, dogs enjoy a variety of foods. However, offering variety can become a complex task.

Navigating the Solution:

Rotating Ingredients: Introduce new ingredients regularly to keep meals interesting and nutritionally diverse.

Seasonal Produce: Take advantage of seasonal fruits and vegetables for freshness and variety.

Challenge 8: The Cost of Ingredients

The cost of purchasing high-quality, fresh ingredients for homemade dog food can add up quickly.

Navigating the Solution:

Budget-Friendly Shopping: Buy in bulk, look for sales, and choose whole foods that offer more nutritional bang for your buck.

Home Gardening: Grow your own vegetables and herbs to include in your dog's meals.

CHAPTER 3: DESIGNING MEALS TAILORED TO YOUR DOG'S DIET

Adapting Recipes by Dog Size and Age

Your dog's energy needs are measured in calories. Factors that affect caloric needs include:

Age: Puppies and young dogs have higher caloric needs for growth, while senior dogs may require fewer calories due to slower metabolism.

Size and Breed: Larger dogs generally need more calories than smaller dogs, but some small breeds are highly energetic and may need more calories pound for pound.

Activity Level: Active and working dogs require more calories than sedentary pets.

Health Status: Dogs with certain health conditions might need more or less energy; for example, dogs with hypothyroidism often require fewer calories.

THE MAGICAL FORMULA FOR CALCULATING THE EXACT AMOUNT OF CALORIES YOUR DOG NEEDS

The Resting Energy Requirement (RER) is essentially the amount of calories your dog needs at rest to perform vital bodily functions such as breathing, circulating blood, and maintaining body temperature. Think of it as the baseline energy needs for your dog's system when at rest. It's a starting point for determining the total daily energy requirements, which can be adjusted based on their activity level, life stage, and health status.

Calculating RER - The Formula

The RER for any dog can be calculated using the following formula:

$$RER = 70 \times (Bodyweight\ in\ kg)^{0.75}$$

Let's break it down:

Start with your dog's weight in kilograms. If you only know it in pounds, divide by 2.2 to convert to kilograms.

Raise the body weight in kilograms to the power of 0.75. This is a standard exponent used in metabolic research for dogs (and many other animals).

Multiply that result by 70.

For example, if your dog weighs 10 kilograms:

$$RER = 70 \times (10kg)^{0.75}$$

$$RER = 70 \times 5.72$$

$$RER \approx 400\ Calories\ per\ day$$

This gives you the amount of calories your dog would need per day if they were doing nothing but resting.

However, your dog does more than just rest. They play, walk, run, and sometimes grow (if they're puppies) or nurse (if they're mothers). The RER is adjusted to account for these factors, giving you the Maintenance Energy Requirement (MER):

- For neutered adult dogs, the RER is often multiplied by a factor ranging from 1.2 to 1.6.
- Active dogs might need an RER multiplied by 2 or more.
- Puppies in growth require more energy, often up to 2.5 times the RER.
- Lactating mothers can require 4 times the RER or even more, depending on the size of the litter.

Remember that RER is influenced by:

- **Body Composition:** A lean dog might need more calories than a dog with more body fat, pound for pound.
- **Age:** Older dogs may have a lower metabolism and thus might need fewer calories.
- **Health Conditions:** Certain conditions can either increase or decrease the RER. For example, a dog with hypothyroidism may have a lower RER.

Small Breed Adult Dog (e.g., Yorkshire Terrier, up to 10 lbs)

Estimated RER Range: 200-275 Calories per day

Example: A 5 lb adult Yorkie might need around 200 Calories per day for basic metabolic functions.

Medium Breed Adult Dog (e.g., Cocker Spaniel, 11-50 lbs)

Estimated RER Range: 350-900 Calories per day

Example: A 30 lb adult Cocker Spaniel could require roughly 600 Calories per day.

Large Breed Adult Dog (e.g., Labrador, Retriever, 51-90 lbs)

Estimated RER Range: 975-1600 Calories per day

Example: A 70 lb adult Lab might need about 1300 Calories per day.

Giant Breed Adult Dog (e.g., Great Dane, over 90 lbs)

Estimated RER Range: 1650+ Calories per day

Example: A 120 lb adult Great Dane could require 1650 Calories or more per day.

Active/Working Dogs (e.g., Border Collie)

Estimated RER Range: May require 2-3 times the RER of a sedentary dog

Example: An active 40 lb Border Collie could require around 1200-1800 Calories per day.

Puppies (up to 4 months old)

Estimated RER Range: Typically requires 3 times the RER of an adult dog

Example: A 15 lb puppy might need around 900 Calories per day during peak growth periods.

Senior Dogs

Estimated RER Range: May require fewer calories than their younger counterparts due to decreased activity

Example: An aging 50 lb dog might need only 700-900 Calories per day, less than during their prime adult years.

Dogs with Specific Conditions (e.g., Overweight, Underweight, or Illness)

Estimated RER Range: Should be calculated specifically by a veterinarian to address the health condition

Example: An overweight 50 lb dog on a weight loss plan might be restricted to around 700 Calories per day under veterinary supervision.

Here's a simple chart based on an average caloric need that you may adjust for homemade diets. Please consult your veterinarian for the most accurate feeding guidelines, especially if your dog has special dietary needs.

Dog's Weight	Cups of Food Per Day (Approx.)
5 lbs	1/2 to 5/8 cup
10 lbs	3/4 to 1 cup
20 lbs	1 1/4 to 1 1/2 cups
30 lbs	1 3/4 to 2 1/4 cups
40 lbs	2 1/4 to 3 cups
50 lbs	2 2/3 to 3 1/3 cups
60 lbs	3 to 4 cups
70 lbs	3 1/2 to 4 1/2 cups
80 lbs	3 3/4 to 5 cups
90 lbs	4 1/4 to 5 1/2 cups
100 lbs	4 1/2 to 6 cups

RER and calorie needs are not static. They change as your dog ages, gains or loses weight, or changes their activity level. You'll need to recalculate RER:

- ◊ After any significant weight loss or gain.
- ◊ As your dog transitions from one life stage to another (puppy to adult, adult to senior).
- ◊ If there's a change in activity level (becomes more active or sedentary).
- ◊ If your dog develops health problems or recovers from illness.

Regular monitoring and consultation with your veterinarian are essential to ensure the RER calculations remain accurate and relevant to your dog's health. Bring your dog in for regular check-ups, including weight checks and discussions about diet. Annual blood work can help detect any internal changes that might affect your dog's RER.

Catering to Picky Eaters

In the doggy dining room, not all guests are easy to please. Picky eaters can turn mealtime into a standoff, where only the most delicious and tempting dishes will be accepted. If your canine companion is more finicky than food-driven, this chapter will guide you through the culinary strategies to satisfy even the most discerning of palates.

First, understand that pickiness can be innate or developed due to habits or past experiences. Some dogs may be picky due to medical issues, so a vet visit is crucial to rule out underlying problems.

Dogs, much like humans, have flavor preferences. While we can't always ask them what they fancy, we can experiment with different proteins, carbs, and fats to discover their favorites.

- **Protein Tango:** Alternate between chicken, beef, lamb, and fish to see which gets the tail wagging.
- **Carb Variety:** Try sweet potatoes, pumpkins, rice, or oats for different textures and flavors.
- **Fats for Flavor:** A drizzle of salmon oil or chicken fat can make meals more appealing.

Some dogs prefer a crunch, while others favor a stew. Varying the texture of your dog's meals can often make a difference. Mix homemade food with a bit of dry kibble for added texture. For those who like it smooth, consider pureeing ingredients for a consistent and creamy texture.

Just like a cold day can make a warm meal more inviting, the temperature of your dog's food can affect their willingness to eat. Gently warm the food to release the aroma, making it more enticing. On hot days, chilled or frozen treats can be more appealing.

The way food is presented can impact a dog's interest in it. Make their dining area pleasant and their meals visually appealing (at least to the canine eye). Create a quiet, distraction-free area for your dog to eat. Sometimes, simply changing the bowl or the way the food is spread out can pique a dog's interest.

Dogs thrive on routine. Consistent feeding times and not leaving food out for grazing can encourage picky eaters to eat when food is offered.

Positive reinforcement can go a long way. Encouraging your dog during mealtime and rewarding them for eating can create positive mealtime associations. Offer verbal praise and petting when your dog eats well. Consider a short play session after meals as a reward for eating.

If you're transitioning to a new food, do it gradually. A sudden change can turn off a picky eater. Mix new food in with the old, slowly increasing the proportion over several days.

If all else fails and you're concerned about nutritional gaps, ensure that your dog gets all their essential nutrients. In some cases, your vet may suggest an appetite stimulant.

Food allergies

When it comes to food, not every ingredient agrees with every dog. Just as in humans, dogs can have allergies that manifest in itchy skin, digestive upset, or other health issues. This chapter addresses the complexities of canine food allergies, how to identify them, and strategies for crafting an allergy-friendly diet.

Food allergies in dogs typically involve an immune response to a protein source in the food, although they can react to any ingredient their body perceives as foreign. When an allergic dog eats the offending food, their body mistakenly identifies the protein as a threat and mounts an immune response, which can result in symptoms such as:

- Itchy skin or recurrent ear infections

- Vomiting or diarrhea
- Chronic gas, coughing, or sneezing
- General malaise or lethargy
- Poor coat quality

The first step in addressing food allergies is to identify what your dog is reacting to. This can be a challenge, as symptoms may not appear for several days after ingestion.

The gold standard for identifying food allergens is an elimination diet. This involves feeding your dog a diet with protein and carbohydrate sources they have never eaten before. Once symptoms resolve, you can reintroduce foods one at a time to determine which causes the allergic reaction.

Another method, though less common for food allergies, is intradermal skin testing, where small amounts of potential allergens are injected into the skin. This method is more frequently used for environmental allergies.

Blood tests can check for antibodies to certain foods, though their reliability for diagnosing food allergies is debated among veterinary professionals.

Once you've identified the allergens, you can start crafting a diet that avoids them. Here are some tips:

- **Novel Proteins:** Use proteins your dog has never eaten before, such as duck, venison, or fish.
- **Limited Ingredients:** Choose diets with as few ingredients as possible to minimize the risk of reactions and make it easier to pinpoint allergens.
- **Home-Cooked Meals:** Preparing meals at home ensures you know exactly what's in your dog's food.
- **Balanced Recipes:** Consult with a veterinary nutritionist to ensure your homemade diet is nutritionally complete.
- **Supplements:** Use supplements if needed to make up for any nutrients that might be missing from a limited ingredient diet.

Transitioning to a new diet should be done gradually over the course of several days. This can help avoid any gastrointestinal upset and make it easier to spot reactions to new ingredients.

Living with food allergies means constant vigilance to avoid accidental exposure to the allergen. This includes:

- **Reading Labels:** Always read labels on commercial dog foods and treats to avoid hidden allergens.
- **Communication:** Inform everyone in the household and any caretakers about your dog's dietary restrictions.
- **Cross-Contamination:** Be aware of cross-contamination risks, especially if you have multiple pets on different diets.

Dealing with food allergies can be a journey full of trials and errors, but finding a diet that alleviates your dog's symptoms is worth the effort. With patience, careful planning, and consultation with your vet or a nutritionist, you can provide a balanced diet that keeps your dog healthy and happy, free from the discomfort of allergic reactions.

Cooking for Dogs with Specific Health Conditions

When a dog faces a health challenge, nutrition often becomes an integral part of the management plan. Cooking for a dog with specific health conditions requires a tailored approach, ensuring that the meals support their medical treatment and overall well-being.

Before changing your dog's diet, it's imperative to consult with your veterinarian or a veterinary nutritionist. They can provide you with a dietary plan that complements your dog's treatment and helps manage their condition.

Common Health Conditions and Dietary Adjustments

Kidney Disease
Dogs with kidney disease benefit from diets low in phosphorus and moderate in high-quality protein. Increased omega-3 fatty acids can help reduce inflammation, and enhanced water intake is crucial to help manage waste removal.

Diabetes
Diabetic dogs require a consistent and controlled diet to maintain stable blood glucose levels. High-fiber diets are often recommended because they can help slow glucose absorption. Complex carbohydrates like sweet potatoes and legumes can be beneficial, while simple sugars should be avoided.

Heart Disease
For dogs with heart disease, lower sodium content is key to reduce fluid build-up. Diets rich in omega-3 fatty acids from fish oil can support heart health, and moderate levels of high-quality protein are essential.

Pancreatitis
Dogs who have experienced pancreatitis often need low-fat diets to reduce the workload on the pancreas. Easily digestible carbohydrates and lean proteins can help meet their nutritional needs without exacerbating the condition.

Allergies
As discussed previously, dogs with food allergies need diets free from the offending allergens. Novel proteins and carbohydrates, or hydrolyzed protein diets where the protein is broken down so the immune system doesn't recognize it, can be helpful.

Obesity
Weight management diets are lower in fat and calories but high in fiber to keep the dog feeling full. Portion control and careful monitoring of caloric intake are essential strategies in cooking for overweight dogs.

Always choose ingredients that are safe for dogs. Avoid toxic foods such as onions, grapes, and chocolate, and be cautious with seasonings, many of which are not dog-friendly. Ensure that all ingredients are fresh and that meals are stored properly to avoid spoilage.

Cook ingredients gently to preserve their nutrients. Steaming and boiling are good methods for vegetables, while baking or grilling lean meats is effective without adding extra fat.

Consistency is critical, particularly for conditions like diabetes. Measure ingredients carefully to ensure that each meal is nutritionally equivalent to the last.

CHAPTER 4: LIFE STAGE RECIPES

Puppy Recipes

BREAKFAST PORRIDGE

Prep Time: 10 minutes | **Cook Time**: 5 minutes | **Total Time**: 15 minutes | **Yield**: 2 servings
Estimated Calories per Serving: 100-120 calories
Ingredients:
- 1 cup rolled oats
- 1 small apple, peeled and finely chopped
- 1 tablespoon ground flaxseed
- 1 teaspoon honey (optional, only for puppies over 12 months)
- 2 cups water

Instructions:
Cook: In a small saucepan, combine all ingredients. Bring to a boil, then reduce heat and simmer, stirring frequently until the oats are soft and the mixture has thickened, about 5 minutes.
Cool: Allow the porridge to cool to room temperature before serving to your puppy.

CHICKEN AND RICE DINNER

Prep Time: 10 minutes | **Cook Time**: 25 minutes | **Total Time**: 35 minutes | **Yield**: 4 servings
Estimated Calories per Serving: 150-170 calories
Ingredients:
- 1 cup cooked, shredded chicken
- 1 cup cooked brown rice
- 1/2 cup peas, cooked
- 1/2 cup carrots, diced and cooked
- 1 tablespoon olive oil

Instructions:
Mix: Combine the chicken, rice, peas, and carrots in a bowl. Drizzle with olive oil and mix well to coat evenly.
Serve: Ensure the mixture is at room temperature before serving to your puppy.

MEATBALL TREATS

Prep Time: 15 minutes | **Cook Time**: 20 minutes | **Total Time**: 35 minutes | **Yield**: 20 meatballs

Estimated Calories per Serving: 30-40 calories

Ingredients:
- 1/2 pound ground turkey or chicken
- 1/4 cup grated carrot
- 1/4 cup cooked quinoa
- 1 egg, beaten

Instructions:

Mix: In a bowl, combine the ground meat, carrot, quinoa, and egg. Mix until well combined.

Shape: Form into small, bite-sized balls.

Cook: Place the meatballs on a baking sheet lined with parchment paper and bake in a preheated oven at 350°F (175°C) for 20 minutes or until cooked through.

Cool: Let them cool before serving as treats or mixing into regular meals.

FISH STEW

Prep Time: 15 minutes | **Cook Time**: 20 minutes | **Total Time**: 35 minutes | **Yield**: 3 servings

Estimated Calories per Serving: 120-140 calories

Ingredients:
- 1/2 pound white fish fillets (e.g., cod, tilapia), chopped into small pieces
- 1 small potato, peeled and cubed
- 1/2 cup chopped spinach
- 1/4 cup peas
- 1 tablespoon olive oil
- 2 cups fish or vegetable broth

Instructions:

Cook: In a pot, heat the olive oil over medium heat. Add the potato cubes and cook until slightly tender.

Simmer: Add the fish, spinach, peas, and broth. Bring to a simmer and cook for 10-15 minutes, until the fish is cooked through and the potatoes are soft.

Serve: Allow the stew to cool to a safe temperature before serving to your puppy.

Adult Recipes

BEEF AND VEGETABLE CASSEROLE

Prep Time: 15 minutes | **Cook Time**: 40 minutes | **Total Time**: 55 minutes | **Yield**: 4 servings

Estimated Calories per Serving: 250-300 calories

Ingredients:
- 1 pound ground beef
- 1 cup brown rice
- 1 cup chopped carrots
- 1 cup chopped green beans
- 1 tablespoon olive oil
- 4 cups beef broth

Instructions:

Brown the beef: In a large pot, heat the olive oil over medium heat. Add the ground beef and cook until browned.

Add rice and vegetables: Stir in the brown rice, carrots, and green beans.

Cook with broth: Pour in the beef broth and bring the mixture to a boil. Reduce heat to low and simmer, covered, for about 30 minutes until the rice is tender and most of the liquid is absorbed.

Cool and serve: Let the casserole cool to room temperature before serving.

CHICKEN AND SWEET POTATO STEW

Prep Time: 10 minutes | **Cook Time**: 30 minutes | **Total Time**: 40 minutes | **Yield**: 4 servings

Estimated Calories per Serving: 200-250 calories

Ingredients:
- 1/2 pound boneless, skinless chicken breasts, cubed
- 2 medium sweet potatoes, peeled and cubed
- 1/2 cup chopped spinach
- 1 tablespoon coconut oil
- 3 cups chicken broth

Instructions:

Cook the chicken: In a large pot, heat the coconut oil over medium heat. Add the chicken and cook until browned.

Simmer with vegetables: Add the sweet potatoes, spinach, and chicken broth. Bring to a simmer and cook for about 20 minutes, until the sweet potatoes are tender.

Cool and serve: Allow the stew to cool before serving to ensure it's safe for your dog to eat.

SALMON AND PEA RISOTTO

Prep Time: 10 minutes | **Cook Time**: 25 minutes | **Total Time**: 35 minutes | **Yield**: 3 servings
Estimated Calories per Serving: 220-270 calories
Ingredients:
- 1 cup arborio rice
- 1/2 pound salmon fillet, skin removed and diced
- 1/2 cup peas
- 1 tablespoon olive oil
- 3 cups fish or vegetable broth

Instructions:
Cook salmon: In a pot, heat the olive oil over medium heat. Add the salmon and cook until it's opaque.
Add rice and broth: Stir in the arborio rice and one cup of broth. Continue to add broth gradually, stirring constantly, until the rice is creamy and al dente, about 20 minutes.
Mix in peas: Add the peas in the last 5 minutes of cooking.
Cool and serve: Let the risotto cool to room temperature before serving.

TURKEY AND PUMPKIN TREATS

Prep Time: 20 minutes | **Cook Time**: 30 minutes | **Total Time**: 50 minutes | **Yield**: 24 treats
Estimated Calories per Serving: 30-40 calories
Ingredients:
- 2 cups whole wheat flour
- 1/2 cup canned pumpkin (ensure it's pure pumpkin, not pie filling)
- 1/2 pound ground turkey, cooked
- 1 egg

Instructions:
Mix ingredients: In a large bowl, combine the whole wheat flour, canned pumpkin, cooked ground turkey, and egg. Stir until well mixed.
Shape treats: Roll out the mixture on a floured surface and cut into desired shapes with cookie cutters.
Bake: Place on a parchment-lined baking sheet and bake at 350°F (175°C) for 30 minutes.
Cool: Allow treats to cool completely before serving to your dog.

Senior Recipes

GENTLE CHICKEN AND OATMEAL DINNER

Prep Time: 10 minutes | **Cook Time**: 20 minutes | **Total Time**: 30 minutes | **Yield**: 3 servings
Estimated Calories per Serving: 200-250 calories
Ingredients:
- 1/2 pound boneless, skinless chicken breasts, finely chopped
- 1 cup rolled oats
- 1/2 cup chopped carrots
- 1 tablespoon olive oil
- 3 cups low-sodium chicken broth

Instructions:
Cook the chicken: In a pot, heat the olive oil over medium heat. Add the chicken and cook until thoroughly done.
Add oats and vegetables: Stir in the rolled oats, carrots, and chicken broth. Bring to a boil, then reduce heat to a simmer and cook until the oats are soft and the carrots are tender, about 15 minutes.
Cool and serve: Allow the mixture to cool to room temperature before serving to your senior dog.

FISH AND POTATO SOFT STEW

Prep Time: 15 minutes | **Cook Time**: 25 minutes | **Total Time**: 40 minutes | **Yield**: 4 servings
Estimated Calories per Serving: 180-230 calories
Ingredients:
- 1/2 pound white fish fillets (such as cod or tilapia), cut into small pieces
- 2 medium potatoes, peeled and cubed
- 1/2 cup chopped green beans
- 1 tablespoon coconut oil
- 3 cups water or low-sodium fish broth

Instructions:
Simmer ingredients: In a pot, heat the coconut oil over medium heat. Add all ingredients and cover with water or broth. Bring to a boil, then reduce heat and simmer until the potatoes are very soft and the fish is fully cooked, about 20 minutes.
Mash lightly: For easier digestion, lightly mash the stew before serving.
Cool and serve: Ensure the stew is at a comfortable temperature before serving to your senior dog.

TURKEY LOAF

Prep Time: 15 minutes | **Cook Time**: 45 minutes | **Total Time**: 1 hour | **Yield**: 5 servings

Estimated Calories per Serving: 250-300 calories

Ingredients:
- 1 pound ground turkey
- 1 egg
- 1/2 cup rolled oats
- 1/4 cup grated carrots
- 1/4 cup finely chopped spinach

Instructions:

Mix ingredients: Combine the ground turkey, egg, rolled oats, carrots, and spinach in a bowl.

Form into loaf: Transfer the mixture into a loaf pan.

Bake: Cook in a preheated oven at 350°F (175°C) for 45 minutes or until the meat is thoroughly cooked.

Cool and slice: Let the loaf cool, then slice into portions appropriate for your dog's size.

SOFT BEEF AND RICE MEAL

Prep Time: 10 minutes | **Cook Time**: 30 minutes | **Total Time**: 40 minutes | **Yield**: 4 servings

Estimated Calories per Serving: 220-270 calories

Ingredients:
- 1/2 pound lean ground beef
- 1 cup cooked white rice
- 1/2 cup pureed pumpkin
- 1/2 cup peas, cooked and mashed

Instructions:

Cook beef: In a skillet, cook the ground beef over medium heat until browned and fully cooked.

Combine with other ingredients: Mix the cooked beef with the white rice, pureed pumpkin, and mashed peas in a bowl.

Warm through: If needed, gently reheat the mixture to enhance flavors and digestibility.

Cool and serve: Allow the meal to cool to a safe temperature before feeding it to your senior dog.

CHAPTER 5: MASTERING MEAL PREP FOR DOGS

Structuring Meals

Just as a well-built house needs a solid blueprint, structuring meals for your dog requires a carefully planned approach to ensure they are nutritionally balanced and complete. In this chapter, we'll delve into the 'architecture' of constructing the perfect canine meal.

Consider your dog's size, age, and activity level to determine how often and how much they should eat.
Puppies: Generally require 3-4 meals per day to support their rapid growth.
Adult Dogs: Typically do well with 2 meals per day.
Senior Dogs: If they have trouble digesting larger quantities at once, they might benefit from smaller, more frequent meals.

Each meal should be portioned to provide the calories your dog needs without leading to weight gain or loss, unless intended as part of a weight management plan.
Measure Accurately: Use a kitchen scale or measuring cups to ensure consistency.
Monitor Weight: Adjust portions as needed based on your dog's body condition and weight changes.

Did you know that dogs can get bored with their food? It's true! Keep their palate excited with a carousel of proteins, carbs, and veggies. It's not just about taste—it's about getting a kaleidoscope of nutrients into their diet.

Including a variety of ingredients ensures a wider range of nutrients and keeps meals interesting for your dog.
Protein Rotation: Rotate between different protein sources to provide a spectrum of amino acids.
Veggie Variety: Different vegetables offer different vitamins, minerals, and types of fiber.
Carb Change-Up: Use various types of carbs to prevent food intolerances and provide diverse energy sources.

Some dogs may require supplements to meet their specific needs, but these should only be added under veterinary guidance.
Joint Support: Glucosamine and chondroitin for dogs with joint issues.
Skin and Coat: Omega-3 fatty acids for skin health and a shiny coat.
Digestive Aids: Probiotics can help support gut health.

Kitchen tools for a canine-friendly kitchen

When it comes to preparing meals for your dog, having the right tools in your kitchen isn't just a luxury—it's a necessity for creating nutritious and delicious meals safely and efficiently. This chapter will guide you through outfitting your kitchen with essential equipment tailored for cooking for your canine companion.

A well-equipped kitchen is the backbone of great homemade dog food. Each tool should be chosen not just for its function, but for its durability and safety in handling your dog's meals.

The Stainless Steel Squadron

- **Mixing Bowls:** Opt for a set of stainless steel mixing bowls that won't trap odors or bacteria and can stand up to vigorous mixing.
- **Pots and Pans:** A reliable set of stainless steel cookware is essential for everything from simmering chicken to steaming veggies.

Precision Instruments

- **Measuring Set:** Accurate measurements ensure that your dog gets the right balance of nutrients. A set of sturdy, stainless steel measuring cups and spoons is crucial.
- **Kitchen Scale:** When a recipe calls for weight measurements, a digital kitchen scale ensures you're providing the right amount of each ingredient.
-

The Prep Brigade

- **Cutting Boards:** Keep separate, color-coded cutting boards: one for meats and one for produce, exclusively for your dog's food preparation to avoid cross-contamination.
- **Quality Knives:** A sharp chef's knife and a smaller paring knife will make prepping ingredients easier and safer.

The Mashing and Pureeing Platoon

- **Blender or Food Processor:** For creating smooth purees that are easier for some dogs to digest or to hide medications in a tasty treat, a reliable blender or food processor is key.

The Slow Cooking Sentinel

- **Slow Cooker:** Ideal for busy pet parents, a slow cooker allows you to cook in bulk and ensure that meats are tender and easy for your dog to eat.

The Treat Workshop

- **Dehydrator:** Perfect for making your own jerky and dehydrated fruits and vegetables, a dehydrator can be a game-changer for healthy snacking.
- **Baking Sheets and Silicone Mats:** For homemade treats, these are indispensable. Silicone baking mats reduce the need for oils and are easy to clean.

The Preservation Unit

- **Airtight Containers:** Quality airtight containers are the guardians of your dog's fresh food, locking in nutrients and flavor until it's time to serve.
- **Serving Scoops:** Pre-measured food scoops tagged with measurements ensure that you're never over or under-feeding.

The Sanitation Squad

- **Dish Brushes and Sponges:** Keeping tools and surfaces clean is paramount, so have dedicated brushes and sponges for your dog's kitchenware.
- **Dishwasher:** If possible, a dishwasher not only saves time but also sanitizes your dog's dishes and cookware effectively.

Safety Measures

- **First Aid Kit:** Accidents can happen, so keep a first aid kit within reach, stocked with items suitable for both you and your pet.

While equipping your kitchen, remember that the goal is to prepare meals that contribute to your dog's health and happiness. Each tool is an investment in their well-being. Cooking for your dog should be approached with the same seriousness as cooking for any family member, ensuring meals are prepared with love, care, and consideration for their specific dietary needs.

In your canine-friendly kitchen, you'll find that preparation and cooking become more than routine—they become an expression of the bond between you and your pet. With these tools, you'll be ready to tackle any recipe and cater to your dog's dietary needs, all while keeping their safety and nutrition front and center.

Cooking methods

Cooking for your dog is an art form that melds nutrition with deliciousness. The methods you choose can affect the flavor, texture, and even the nutritional content of the food. This chapter is devoted to the various cooking methods suitable for preparing dog-friendly meals that are both wholesome and enticing.

Steaming: The Gentle Touch

Steaming is a cooking method that preserves the integrity of vitamins and minerals in vegetables and meats. It's gentle, keeping foods moist and digestible, which is ideal for dogs with sensitive stomachs.

- ◊ **Pro Tip:** Use a steamer basket over a pot of boiling water, and steam until the food reaches the desired tenderness.

Boiling: The Simple Solution

Boiling is a straightforward method, especially good for making stews and broths. However, some nutrients, especially water-soluble vitamins, can be lost in the cooking water.

- ◊ **Nutrition Note:** To retain the nutrients when boiling vegetables, use as little water as possible and consider incorporating the cooking water into your dog's meal.

Baking: The Flavor Enhancer

Baking can intensify the flavors of meats and vegetables without the need for additional fats or oils. It's a hands-off method that allows you to prepare large batches of food at once.

- ◊ **Health Hint:** To prevent dryness, cover the food with foil and bake until just cooked through to retain moisture.

Grilling: The Aromatic Appeal

Grilling imparts a smoky flavor that many dogs love. It can be a healthy way to cook meat, allowing fat to drip away from the food.

- ◊ **Safety First:** Ensure all foods are grilled to a safe temperature and avoid charring, which can be harmful to your dog.

Slow Cooking: The Time Saver

The slow cooker is a busy pet parent's best friend. It allows for the slow infusion of flavors and makes even the toughest cuts of meat fork-tender. Plus, it's a great way to cook in bulk and have meals ready for the week.

- ◊ **Convenience Key:** Prepare all your ingredients, place them in the slow cooker, and let it do the work for you while you tend to other tasks.

Sautéing: Quick and Effective

Sautéing is a quick method that can bring out the natural flavors of foods like chicken, turkey, and vegetables. It requires minimal oil and delivers a pleasing texture and taste.

- ◊ **Cooking Tip:** Use a non-stick pan to reduce the amount of oil needed and keep the heat moderate to avoid burning.

Cooling: Serving it Right

Remember that the temperature at which you serve your dog's food matters. Allow cooked food to cool to room temperature to avoid burning your dog's mouth.

Storage: Saving for Later

Proper storage is as important as the cooking itself. Cool the food quickly, then refrigerate or freeze it in sealed containers to keep it fresh and safe.

Balancing Act: Combining Methods

Don't be afraid to combine cooking methods. You might steam vegetables, grill chicken, and then mix them into a stew you've slowly simmered. This variety can make meals more interesting and appetizing for your dog.

The way you cook your dog's meals is an extension of your care and love. Whether you're gently steaming, slowly stewing, or quickly sautéing, each method contributes to the health and enjoyment of your dog's diet. Remember, though, that the most important ingredients you can offer are the love and attention that go into the preparation of each dish.

Meal prepping tips

In the hustle and bustle of modern life, meal prepping for your canine companion can be a game-changer. It ensures they receive the necessary nutrition without compromising on quality due to a time crunch.

Start with a weekly menu, just like you might for other family members. This plan should incorporate variety and account for your dog's specific nutritional needs. It's a good idea to batch cook proteins, carbs, and veggies that can be mixed and matched throughout the week.

Armed with your meal plan, create a shopping list. Focus on whole, fresh ingredients, and remember that buying in bulk can save time and money. Also, consider your storage capacity—both fridge and freezer space.

Choose a day to be your meal prep day. For many, this is a weekend day when you can devote a couple of hours to cooking.

- ◊ **Pro Tip:** Clean and prep all your ingredients first. Chop veggies, trim meats, and get everything ready to cook.

Batch Cooking: Cook large quantities of a few staple ingredients. Grains like brown rice or proteins like chicken can be cooked in bulk and used throughout the week.

Create an assembly line for meal construction. Pre-measure portions of proteins, carbs, and veggies, and combine them based on your dog's dietary needs.

Storage Containers: Invest in quality storage containers that will keep the food fresh. Pre-portion the meals into daily servings for easy feeding.

Labeling: Label each container with the date and contents. This helps you keep track of what to feed when, especially if you're varying the meals.

When cooking, consider methods that retain nutrients and are efficient for large batches. Steaming and roasting are excellent options.

Cooling Down: Let the food cool completely before packing it away to prevent bacterial growth.

Freezing Techniques: If you're freezing meals, lay them flat in the freezer to save space and allow for quicker thawing.

Plan ahead for thawing. Transfer the next day's meal from the freezer to the fridge the night before, ensuring it's thawed safely by mealtime.

Thawing Tip: Never thaw dog food on the counter at room temperature as it can encourage bacterial growth.

When it's time to serve, you can add fresh elements to the prepped base—like a spoonful of cottage cheese or a sprinkle of herbs for added nutrition and interest.

Keep your prep space clean and organized. Clean as you go, and make sure all utensils and surfaces are washed thoroughly at the end of your prep session.

Even with a plan, be open to improvisation. If you have extra veggies or a bit of leftover cooked meat, find a way to incorporate it into your dog's meals.

Meal prepping for your dog doesn't have to be a chore; it can be a labor of love that's also practical. With these tips, you'll be able to whip up a week's worth of meals, ensuring your furry friend is well-fed with nutritious, homemade food every day of the week.

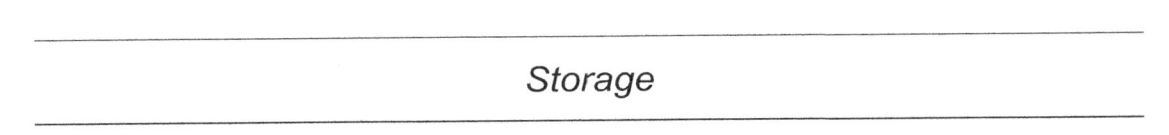

Storage

Proper storage is crucial to maintaining the freshness, nutritional value, and safety of your homemade dog food. In this chapter, we delve into effective storage techniques that prevent spoilage, retain nutrient quality, and ensure that every meal you serve is as healthy and delicious as when it was first prepared.

Food safety begins with proper handling and extends to how you store your dog's meals. Here are the foundational principles:

- **Cooling Down:** Always allow cooked food to cool to room temperature before storing to prevent the growth of harmful bacteria.
- **Separation:** Store dog food separately from human food to avoid cross-contamination.

Selecting the right storage containers can make a significant difference in preserving the quality of food:

Material: BPA-free plastic, glass, or stainless steel containers are best for food storage. Glass is ideal for visibility and safety, while BPA-free plastic is lightweight and often more convenient.

Airtight Seals: Choose containers with airtight seals to keep food fresh and protect it from bacteria and freezer burn.

Size Variety: Have a variety of sizes to accommodate different portions, ensuring that each meal is packed neatly without excessive air space which can lead to freezer burn.

Refrigeration is suitable for short-term storage of homemade dog food.

Most homemade dog foods can be safely stored in the refrigerator for up to 5 days. Use a dedicated shelf or area in your refrigerator for dog food to avoid accidental human consumption and to keep the food away from fresh produce.

For ingredients like grains or nutritional supplements that are used in preparing your dog's food, store grains and dry supplements in a cool, dry place away from direct sunlight. Use airtight containers to protect them from moisture and pests.

If your dog doesn't finish their meal, how you handle leftovers is important:

- **Cooling and Storing:** Cool leftovers quickly and store them in the refrigerator.
- **Reuse:** Safely reuse leftovers within 2-3 days, reheating them to the appropriate temperature before serving.

Make it a habit to check your storage areas regularly:
Look for any signs of spoilage such as mold, unusual odors, or discoloration before serving food that has been stored. Keep an inventory to use the oldest products first and avoid waste.

Mistakes to avoid

Cooking for your dog offers numerous benefits, including control over ingredients and the joy of providing a homemade meal. However, as with any venture, there are potential mistakes that can undermine your efforts.

Mistake 1: Nutritional Imbalances
One of the most common and critical errors when cooking for dogs is failing to provide a nutritionally balanced diet.

How to Avoid:

- **Consult a Veterinarian or Canine Nutritionist:** Before starting on homemade meals, speak with a professional to understand the specific nutritional needs of your breed and age of dog.
- **Follow Balanced Recipes:** Use recipes formulated by experts. Resist the urge to make significant adjustments unless advised by a professional.

Mistake 2: Using Unsafe or Toxic Ingredients
Some foods that are perfectly safe for humans can be harmful to dogs.

How to Avoid:

- **Educate Yourself on Unsafe Foods:** Familiarize yourself with foods that are toxic to dogs, such as onions, garlic, grapes, raisins, chocolate, and xylitol, among others.
- **Check All Ingredients:** Always double-check ingredients in recipes to ensure they are safe for canine consumption.

Mistake 3: Inadequate Portion Sizes
Feeding your dog too much or too little can lead to weight issues and associated health problems.

How to Avoid:

- **Measure Food Carefully:** Use a kitchen scale or measuring cups to ensure accurate portion sizes.
- **Monitor Your Dog's Weight:** Adjust portions based on your dog's activity level, weight changes, and health status.

Mistake 4: Lack of Variety
Relying too heavily on one type of food or ingredient can lead to deficiencies or excesses in certain nutrients.

How to Avoid:

- **Rotate Ingredients:** Incorporate a variety of protein sources, vegetables, and grains to ensure a broad spectrum of nutrients.
- **Supplement Wisely:** Depending on your dog's diet, you may need to add specific supplements to prevent deficiencies. Consult with a professional for guidance.

Mistake 5: Improper Food Handling and Storage
Improper handling and storage can lead to foodborne illnesses.

How to Avoid:

- **Practice Good Hygiene:** Always wash your hands before and after handling dog food ingredients.
- **Store Food Properly:** Cool food quickly and refrigerate or freeze it in appropriate portions. Use airtight containers to protect food quality.

Mistake 6: Over-reliance on Supplements
While supplements can be crucial for filling nutritional gaps, relying too heavily on them can lead to other health issues.

How to Avoid:

- **Balance Diet First:** Aim to meet nutritional needs through diet first, using supplements only to fill unavoidable gaps.
- **Consult Professionals:** Before starting any supplements, discuss them with your vet to ensure they are necessary and given in the correct dosages.

Mistake 7: Not Adjusting Diets for Health Changes
Dogs' nutritional needs can change due to age, health conditions, or activity levels. Not adjusting their diet accordingly can lead to health issues.

How to Avoid:

- **Regular Vet Check-ups:** Schedule regular veterinary check-ups to assess your dog's health and dietary needs.
- **Stay Informed:** Keep yourself updated on how nutritional needs can change with age and health status, and adjust the diet as needed.

Mistake 8: Ignoring Signs of Food Intolerances or Allergies
Some dogs may develop allergies or intolerances to certain foods, which can manifest as skin irritations, gastrointestinal disturbances, or other health issues.

How to Avoid:

- **Monitor Reactions:** Pay close attention to any changes in your dog's health or behavior after meals.
- **Elimination Diets:** If you suspect a food allergy or intolerance, consult with your vet about conducting an elimination diet to identify the culprit.

Mistake 9: Inconsistent Meal Preparation

Inconsistent preparation, such as varying ingredient types, cooking methods, or meal times, can affect your dog's digestion and appetite.

How to Avoid:

- **Establish a Routine:** Stick to a consistent routine in both the timing of meals and their preparation.
- **Prep in Batches:** Consider preparing meals in batches under consistent conditions to ensure uniformity and save time

Mistake 10: Neglecting Hydration

Not providing enough fresh water, especially when feeding dry or heavily processed foods, can lead to dehydration.

How to Avoid:

- **Provide Constant Water Access:** Ensure your dog has access to clean water at all times.
- **Include Moist Foods:** Incorporate moist foods in your dog's diet to aid hydration.

10 Secret Ingredients for Shiny Coat and Fresh Breath

1. Omega-3 Fatty Acids (Fish Oil)
Omega-3s, found abundantly in fish oil, are renowned for their ability to improve skin health, leading to a shinier and healthier coat. They also have anti-inflammatory properties that can help keep skin irritations at bay.

2. Coconut Oil
When added sparingly to your dog's diet, coconut oil can enhance the coat's shine and aid in creating a barrier against parasites. It also helps freshen breath and can help control plaque buildup when used in moderation.

3. Parsley
This common herb is not just a garnish. Parsley is famous for its breath-freshening properties and is a natural source of antioxidants, which can support a healthy immune system and a vibrant coat.

4. Flaxseeds
Flaxseeds are a good source of omega-3 fatty acids but from a plant-based origin. They're great for promoting skin and coat health and can be ground and added to your dog's meals to aid in digestion.

5. Carrots
Crunchy and naturally sweet, carrots are excellent for your dog's teeth, helping to mechanically scrub away plaque. They also contain beta-carotene, which may help contribute to a vibrant, healthy coat.

6. Eggs
Eggs are a near-perfect food, rich in highly digestible protein and biotin. These nutrients are essential for a glossy coat and healthy skin. Feeding your dog a hard-boiled or scrambled egg can make a noticeable difference.

7. Chia Seeds
Like flaxseeds, chia seeds are rich in omega-3 fatty acids and have been shown to improve coat shine and skin health. They also help in hydration, which can be beneficial for skin elasticity.

8. Sweet Potatoes
Sweet potatoes are high in vitamin A, which is crucial for skin health. They're also gentle on the digestive system and help add fiber to your dog's diet.

9. Apple Slices

Fresh apple slices can help clean residue off a dog's teeth, freshening breath. They're also a good source of vitamins, including vitamin C, which supports the immune system for overall skin health.

10. Mint

Mint has natural breath-freshening properties and can be added in small amounts to your dog's meals. It's also soothing for the digestive tract and can help aid digestion.

Part 2: Scrumptious Recipes

Treats and rewards

CARROT AND APPLE TREATS

Prep Time: 15 minutes | **Cook Time:** 30 minutes | **Total Time:** 45 minutes | **Yield:** 24 treats
Estimated calories per treat: 60-70 calories
Ingredients:

- 2 1/2 cups whole wheat flour (or substitute with oat or coconut flour for a grain-free option)
- 1/2 cup unsweetened applesauce
- 1/2 cup finely grated carrot
- 1 egg
- 1 tablespoon coconut oil

Instructions:
Mix: In a large bowl, combine the whole wheat flour, unsweetened applesauce, finely grated carrot, egg, and coconut oil. Stir until the mixture forms a dough.
Shape: Roll out the dough on a lightly floured surface to about 1/4 inch thick. Use cookie cutters to cut into desired shapes.
Bake: Place the cut-out treats on a baking sheet lined with parchment paper. Bake in a preheated oven at 350°F (175°C) for 30 minutes, or until crispy.
Cool: Let the treats cool completely on a wire rack before serving to your dog.

SPINACH, CARROT, AND ZUCCHINI TREATS

Prep Time: 20 minutes | **Cook Time:** 25-30 minutes | **Total Time:** 45-50 minutes | **Yield:** 30 treats
Estimated calories per treat: 70-80 calories
Ingredients:

- 1 cup pumpkin puree
- 1/4 cup peanut butter (ensure it's xylitol-free)
- 2 eggs
- 1/2 cup oats
- 3 cups whole wheat flour
- 1 carrot, shredded
- 1 zucchini, shredded
- 1 cup baby spinach, chopped

Instructions:

Mix: In a large bowl, combine pumpkin puree, peanut butter, eggs, and oats. Gradually add in the whole wheat flour until the mixture forms a dough. Fold in the shredded carrot, zucchini, and chopped spinach.
Shape: Roll the dough on a floured surface and cut out treats with cookie cutters.
Bake: Arrange the treats on a parchment-lined baking sheet and bake at 350°F (175°C) for 25-30 minutes, until golden.
Cool: Allow treats to cool before serving to your dog.

SWEET POTATO CHEWIES

Prep Time: 10 minutes | **Cook Time:** 2-3 hours | **Total Time:** About 3 hours 10 minutes | **Yield:** Varies
Estimated calories per treat: 70-80 calories
Ingredients:

- 1 large sweet potato, thinly sliced

Instructions:
Prepare: Arrange the sweet potato slices in a single layer on a baking sheet lined with parchment paper.
Bake: Bake at 250°F (120°C) for 2-3 hours, flipping halfway through, until they are dry and chewy.
Cool: Let the chewies cool before offering them to your dog as a healthy snack.

PEANUT BUTTER AND PUMPKIN DOG TREATS

Prep Time: 10 minutes | **Cook Time:** 40 minutes | **Total Time:** 50 minutes | **Yield:** Varies depending on cutter size

Estimated calories per treat: 50 calories

Ingredients:
- 2 1/2 cups whole wheat flour (or substitute as needed)
- 2 eggs
- 1/2 cup canned pumpkin (ensure it's pure pumpkin)
- 2 tablespoons peanut butter (xylitol-free)
- 1/2 teaspoon salt
- 1/2 teaspoon ground cinnamon

Instructions:

Mix: In a large bowl, combine all the ingredients until a dough forms.
Shape: On a floured surface, roll the dough to about 1/2 inch thickness. Use cookie cutters to cut into shapes.
Bake: Arrange on a baking sheet and bake at 350°F (175°C) for about 40 minutes, or until treats are hard.
Cool: Let the treats cool before serving to your dog.

CHICKEN AND RICE DOG BISCUITS

Prep Time: 15 minutes | **Cook Time:** 20 minutes | **Total Time:** 35 minutes | **Yield:** 24 biscuits

Estimated calories per treat: 50 calories

Ingredients:
- 2 cups brown rice flour
- 1/2 cup cooked, finely diced chicken
- 1 cup cooked rice
- 1 tablespoon parsley
- 1 egg

Instructions:

Preheat: Oven to 325°F (165°C).
Combine: In a bowl, mix all ingredients until well incorporated.
Form: Roll the mixture into small balls and place on a baking sheet. Flatten each with a fork.
Bake: For about 20 minutes, or until they start to brown.
Cool: Allow to cool before serving to your pet.

SWEET POTATO FRIES FOR DOGS

Prep Time: 10 minutes | **Cook Time:** 20 minutes | **Total Time:** 30 minutes | **Yield:** Varies
Estimated calories per treat: 12 calories
Ingredients:

- 1 large sweet potato
- 1 tablespoon coconut oil (melted)
- A sprinkle of turmeric or cinnamon (optional)

Instructions:
Preheat: Oven to 425°F (220°C).
Prepare: Slice the sweet potato into thin fries. Toss with melted coconut oil and optional spices.
Bake: Spread on a baking sheet and bake for about 20 minutes, flipping halfway through.
Cool: Let the fries cool before serving to your dog.

BEEF AND VEGGIE BALLS

Prep Time: 15 minutes | **Cook Time:** 15 minutes | **Total Time:** 30 minutes | **Yield:** 20 balls
Estimated calories per treat: 50 calories
Ingredients:

- 1 pound lean ground beef
- 1/2 cup cooked carrots, mashed
- 1/2 cup cooked peas
- 2 tablespoons grated Parmesan cheese

Instructions:
Preheat: Oven to 400°F (200°C).
Mix: Combine all ingredients in a bowl until evenly mixed.
Form: Shape the mixture into small balls and arrange on a baking sheet.
Bake: For about 15 minutes or until cooked through.
Cool: Allow to cool before serving.

FROZEN YOGURT POPS

Prep Time: 5 minutes | **Freeze Time:** 4 hours | **Total Time:** 4 hours 5 minutes | **Yield:** Varies based on mold size
Estimated calories per treat: 30 calories
Ingredients:
- 2 cups plain, unsweetened yogurt
- 1 banana, mashed
- 1 tablespoon honey (optional)

Instructions:
Mix: Combine all ingredients in a bowl until smooth.
Pour: Into ice cube trays or silicone molds.
Freeze: Until solid, about 4 hours.
Serve: Pop out a frozen yogurt treat for your dog on a warm day.

TURKEY AND SWEET POTATO MEATBALLS

Prep Time: 15 minutes | **Cook Time:** 20 minutes | **Total Time:** 35 minutes | **Yield:** 20-25 meatballs
Estimated calories per treat: 50 calories
Ingredients:
- 1 pound ground turkey
- 1 cup cooked, mashed sweet potato
- 1 egg
- 2 tablespoons chopped parsley
- 1/2 cup oat flour (or finely ground oats)

Instructions:
Preheat: Oven to 375°F (190°C).
Combine: In a bowl, mix together the ground turkey, mashed sweet potato, egg, parsley, and oat flour until well blended.
Form: Shape the mixture into small meatballs and place them on a parchment-lined baking sheet.
Bake: For 20 minutes, or until the meatballs are cooked through.
Cool: Let them cool before offering to your dog.

APPLE CINNAMON COOKIES

Prep Time: 10 minutes | **Cook Time:** 30 minutes | **Total Time:** 40 minutes | **Yield:** 2 dozen cookies
Estimated calories per treat: 60 calories
Ingredients:

- 2 cups whole wheat flour (or substitute as needed)
- 1/2 cup unsweetened applesauce
- 1 egg
- 2 tablespoons coconut oil
- 1 teaspoon ground cinnamon

Instructions:
Preheat: Oven to 350°F (175°C).
Mix: Combine all ingredients in a bowl until a dough forms.
Roll: On a floured surface, roll out the dough and use cookie cutters to cut into shapes.
Bake: Place on a baking sheet and bake for 30 minutes, or until golden and crispy.
Cool: Allow to cool before serving.

SALMON AND SWEET PEA TREATS

Prep Time: 15 minutes | **Cook Time:** 20 minutes | **Total Time:** 35 minutes | **Yield:** 24 treats
Estimated calories per treat: 40 calories
Ingredients:

- 1 can (about 6 oz) salmon, undrained
- 1 cup cooked peas
- 1 egg
- 1 cup whole wheat flour

Instructions:
Preheat: Oven to 350°F (175°C).
Blend: In a food processor, blend the salmon, peas, and egg until smooth.
Combine: Transfer to a bowl and mix in the flour to form a dough.
Shape: Roll out the dough and cut into shapes with a cookie cutter.
Bake: Arrange on a lined baking sheet and bake for 20 minutes.
Cool: Let the treats cool before serving.

BEEFY SQUASH BITES

Prep Time: 20 minutes | **Cook Time:** 25 minutes | **Total Time:** 45 minutes | **Yield:** 30 bites
Estimated calories per treat: 30 calories

Ingredients:
- 1/2 pound lean ground beef
- 1 cup grated zucchini or yellow squash
- 1 egg
- 1 cup whole wheat flour

Instructions:

Preheat: Oven to 350°F (175°C).
Combine: Mix the ground beef, grated squash, egg, and flour in a bowl until well combined.
Form: Shape into small, bite-sized balls and place on a parchment paper-lined baking sheet.
Bake: For 25 minutes or until firm and slightly browned.
Cool: Allow to cool before serving to your pet.

CHEESY VEGGIE MUFFINS

Prep Time: 15 minutes | **Cook Time:** 25 minutes | **Total Time:** 40 minutes | **Yield:** 12 muffins
Estimated Calories per Muffin: 100-120 calories

Ingredients:
- 2 cups whole wheat flour (or substitute as needed)
- 1/2 cup shredded cheese (choose a low-fat option)
- 1 cup mixed vegetables (carrots, peas, and spinach), cooked and pureed
- 1 egg
- 1 cup water

Instructions:

Preheat: Oven to 350°F (175°C) and grease a muffin tin.
Combine: Mix all ingredients in a large bowl until well combined.
Fill: Spoon the mixture into the muffin tins, filling each cup about 3/4 full.
Bake: For 25 minutes or until a toothpick comes out clean.
Cool: Allow the muffins to cool before serving to your dog.

APPLE AND OATMEAL DOG SNACKS

Prep Time: 10 minutes | **Cook Time:** 20 minutes | **Total Time:** 30 minutes | **Yield:** 2 dozen snacks
Estimated Calories per Snack: 30-40 calories
Ingredients:

- 1 cup unsweetened applesauce
- 1 egg
- 1/2 cup rolled oats
- 3 cups whole wheat flour (or substitute as needed)
- 2 tablespoons honey (optional)

Instructions:
Preheat: Oven to 350°F (175°C).
Mix: Combine applesauce, egg, oats, flour, and honey in a bowl until a dough forms.
Roll and Cut: Roll out the dough and use cookie cutters to create fun shapes.
Bake: Place on a parchment-lined baking sheet and bake for 20 minutes or until edges are golden.
Cool: Allow snacks to cool before serving.

CHICKEN AND PARSLEY BITES

Prep Time: 15 minutes | **Cook Time:** 25 minutes | **Total Time:** 40 minutes | **Yield:** 20-30 treats
Estimated Calories per Treat: 20-30 calories
Ingredients:

- 1 cup cooked, finely chopped chicken
- 1 cup whole wheat flour (or substitute with coconut flour for a grain-free option)
- 1/4 cup finely chopped parsley
- 1 egg
- 1 tablespoon olive oil
- 2 tablespoons water (or more, as needed)

Instructions:
Preheat your oven to 350°F (175°C). Line a baking sheet with parchment paper.
Combine ingredients: In a large mixing bowl, combine the finely chopped chicken, whole wheat flour, chopped parsley, egg, and olive oil. Add water gradually and mix until the dough is cohesive and slightly sticky. You may need to adjust the amount of water depending on the absorbency of the flour.
Shape the treats: Pinch off small pieces of the dough and roll them into balls about the size of a marble. Place them on the prepared baking sheet, flattening each ball slightly with the back of a spoon or your fingers.
Bake: Bake in the preheated oven for 20-25 minutes, or until the treats are golden and firm to the touch.
Cool: Allow the treats to cool on the baking sheet for 10 minutes before transferring them to a wire rack to cool completely.

Soups and broth

CHICKEN AND PUMPKIN BROTH

Prep Time: 15 minutes | **Cook Time:** 30 minutes | **Total Time:** 45 minutes | **Yield:** Varies depending on serving size

Estimated calories per serving: 25 calories

Ingredients:
- 1 chicken breast (skinless and boneless)
- 1 cup pumpkin puree (ensure it's pure pumpkin)
- 1 carrot, chopped
- 4 cups water

Instructions:

Mix: In a large pot, combine the chicken breast, chopped carrot, and water.
Cook: Bring to a boil, then reduce heat and simmer for 30 minutes, or until the chicken is fully cooked.
Prepare: Remove the chicken from the pot, allow it to cool, then shred into small, bite-sized pieces.
Blend: Stir the pumpkin puree into the broth until well mixed. Add the shredded chicken back into the pot.
Serve: Allow the broth to cool to room temperature before serving a suitable amount to your dog.

BEEF AND SWEET POTATO SOUP

Prep Time: 20 minutes | **Cook Time:** 40 minutes | **Total Time:** 1 hour | **Yield:** Varies depending on serving size

Estimated calories per serving: 40 calories

Ingredients:
- 1/2 pound lean ground beef
- 1 large sweet potato, cubed
- 1/2 cup chopped carrots
- 4 cups beef broth or water

Instructions:

Brown: In a large pot, cook the ground beef over medium heat until browned.
Combine: Add the sweet potato cubes, chopped carrots, and beef broth to the pot.
Simmer: Bring to a boil, then reduce heat and simmer for 40 minutes, or until vegetables are soft.
Cool: Allow the soup to cool to room temperature before serving a small portion to your dog.

TURKEY AND RICE COMFORT SOUP

Prep Time: 15 minutes | **Cook Time:** 25 minutes | **Total Time:** 40 minutes | **Yield:** Varies depending on serving size

Estimated calories per serving: 30 calories

Ingredients:

- 1/2 pound ground turkey, cooked
- 1 cup cooked brown rice
- 1 carrot, finely chopped
- 3 cups low-sodium chicken or turkey broth

Instructions:

Cook: In a large pot, thoroughly cook the ground turkey.

Combine: Add the cooked brown rice, finely chopped carrot, and broth to the pot with the turkey.

Simmer: Bring the mixture to a boil, then reduce the heat and simmer for about 20 minutes, or until the carrots are tender.

Cool: Allow the soup to cool to room temperature before serving to your dog.

FISH AND PARSLEY STEW

Prep Time: 10 minutes | **Cook Time:** 20 minutes | **Total Time:** 30 minutes | **Yield:** Varies depending on serving size

Estimated calories per serving: 35 calories

Ingredients:

- 1/2 pound white fish (e.g., cod or tilapia), cooked and flaked
- 1/2 cup chopped parsley
- 3 cups water
- 1 tablespoon olive oil

Instructions:

Prepare: Cook the fish thoroughly, then flake it apart.

Simmer: In a pot, combine the flaked fish, chopped parsley, water, and olive oil. Simmer for 20 minutes over low heat.

Cool: Ensure the stew cools down to room temperature before serving a small portion to your dog.

VEGGIE BROTH DELIGHT

Prep Time: 10 minutes | **Cook Time:** 1 hour | **Total Time:** 1 hour 10 minutes | **Yield:** Varies depending on serving size

Estimated calories per serving: 15 calories

Ingredients:
- 1 cup chopped kale
- 1/2 cup sliced carrots
- 1/2 cup chopped celery
- 4 cups water

Instructions:

Combine: In a large pot, add the kale, carrots, celery, and water.

Simmer: Bring to a boil, then reduce heat and simmer for 1 hour to allow the flavors to meld.

Strain: Remove the vegetables (optional) and allow the broth to cool to room temperature before serving.

CHICKEN AND BARLEY BROTH

Prep Time: 15 minutes | **Cook Time:** 1 hour | **Total Time:** 1 hour 15 minutes | **Yield:** Varies depending on serving size

Estimated calories per serving: 40 calories

Ingredients:
- 1 chicken breast, boneless and skinless
- 1/2 cup barley
- 1 carrot, chopped
- 4 cups low-sodium chicken broth

Instructions:

Cook: Place the chicken breast in a pot with the barley, carrot, and chicken broth.

Simmer: Bring to a boil, then reduce heat and simmer for about 1 hour, or until the barley is tender and the chicken is fully cooked.

Shred: Remove the chicken, let it cool, then shred it and add it back to the pot. Allow cooling before serving.

BEEFY VEGGIE SOUP

Prep Time: 20 minutes | **Cook Time:** 30 minutes | **Total Time:** 50 minutes | **Yield:** Varies depending on serving size

Estimated calories per serving: 45 calories

Ingredients:

- 1/2 pound lean ground beef
- 1/2 cup diced sweet potatoes
- 1/2 cup chopped green beans
- 4 cups beef or vegetable broth

Instructions:

Brown: In a pot, cook the ground beef until no longer pink.

Add Veggies: Add the sweet potatoes, green beans, and broth to the pot.

Simmer: Bring to a boil, then simmer for about 30 minutes, or until the vegetables are tender.

Cool: Let the soup cool to room temperature before serving to your pet.

LAMB AND MINT SOUP

Prep Time: 15 minutes | **Cook Time:** 40 minutes | **Total Time:** 55 minutes | **Yield:** Varies depending on serving size

Estimated calories per serving: 50 calories

Ingredients:

- 1/2 pound ground lamb
- 1 cup diced carrots
- 1/4 cup fresh mint leaves, finely chopped
- 4 cups water or low-sodium beef broth

Instructions:

Brown Lamb: In a pot, cook the ground lamb over medium heat until fully browned.

Simmer: Add the diced carrots, mint leaves, and water or broth to the pot with the lamb. Bring to a boil, then reduce heat and let it simmer for about 40 minutes.

Cool: Ensure the soup is cool to room temperature before serving to your dog. The mint will provide a refreshing flavor that many dogs enjoy.

QUINOA VEGETABLE STEW

Prep Time: 10 minutes | **Cook Time:** 25 minutes | **Total Time:** 35 minutes | **Yield:** Varies depending on serving size

Estimated calories per serving: 30 calories

Ingredients:

- 1/2 cup quinoa, rinsed
- 1 cup chopped kale
- 1/2 cup chopped carrots
- 1/2 cup chopped zucchini
- 4 cups low-sodium vegetable broth

Instructions:

Cook Quinoa: In a pot, add the quinoa and vegetable broth, and bring to a boil. Reduce heat to low, cover, and simmer for 15 minutes.

Add Vegetables: Stir in the kale, carrots, and zucchini. Continue to simmer for an additional 10 minutes, or until the vegetables are tender.

Cool: Allow the stew to cool to room temperature before offering it to your dog. This stew is a great source of protein and vitamins for your pet.

DUCK AND PEAR PUREE

Prep Time: 10 minutes | **Cook Time:** 30 minutes | **Total Time:** 40 minutes | **Yield:** Varies depending on serving size

Estimated calories per serving: 60 calories

Ingredients:

- 1 duck breast, skinless
- 1 ripe pear, cored and chopped
- 1 tablespoon honey (optional, skip if your dog is sensitive to sugars)
- 3 cups water

Instructions:

Cook Duck: Place the duck breast in a pot with water. Bring to a boil, then reduce heat and simmer for about 20-25 minutes, or until the duck is fully cooked.

Blend: Remove the duck from the water and let it cool. In a blender, puree the cooked duck, chopped pear, and honey (if using) until smooth. You can add a bit of the cooking water to adjust the consistency.

Serve: Allow the puree to cool to room temperature before serving. This is especially suitable for older dogs or those with dental issues, offering a soft and flavorful treat.

Seafood recipes

SALMON AND SWEET POTATO JERKY

Prep Time: 15 minutes | **Cook Time:** 3 hours | **Total Time:** 3 hours 15 minutes | **Yield:** Varies
Estimated calories per treat: 30 calories
Ingredients:

- 1/2 pound fresh salmon, skinless
- 1 large sweet potato, thinly sliced
- A pinch of turmeric (optional)

Instructions:
Prepare: Preheat your oven to 175°F (80°C). Line a baking sheet with parchment paper.
Slice: Cut the salmon into thin strips, similar in thickness to the sweet potato slices.
Season: Optionally, sprinkle a tiny bit of turmeric on the salmon and sweet potato slices for extra health benefits.
Arrange: Place the salmon strips and sweet potato slices on the prepared baking sheet, ensuring they don't overlap.
Bake: Dehydrate in the oven for about 3 hours, or until the jerky is dry and chewy.
Cool: Allow the jerky to cool completely before serving to your dog.

TUNA AND PARSLEY BISCUITS

Prep Time: 20 minutes | **Cook Time:** 25 minutes | **Total Time**: 45 minutes | **Yield:** 24 biscuits
Estimated calories per biscuit: 50 calories
Ingredients:

- 1 can (about 6 oz) tuna in water, drained
- 2 cups whole wheat flour (substitute as needed)
- 1 egg
- 1/4 cup fresh parsley, chopped
- 1/2 cup water

Instructions:
Preheat: Your oven to 350°F (175°C).
Mix: In a large bowl, combine the tuna, flour, egg, parsley, and water until a dough forms.
Roll Out: On a floured surface, roll the dough to about 1/4 inch thick. Use cookie cutters to cut into shapes.
Bake: Place the biscuits on a parchment-lined baking sheet and bake for 25 minutes, or until golden.
Cool: Let the biscuits cool before treating your dog.

SHRIMP AND RICE BALLS

Prep Time: 15 minutes | **Cook Time:** 30 minutes | **Total Time:** 45 minutes | **Yield:** 20 balls

Estimated calories per ball: 25 calories

Ingredients:
- 1/2 pound shrimp, cooked and finely chopped
- 1 cup cooked brown rice
- 1 egg, beaten
- 1 tablespoon finely chopped dill

Instructions:

Preheat: Your oven to 350°F (175°C).

Combine: In a bowl, mix the shrimp, brown rice, egg, and dill until well blended.

Form Balls: Scoop the mixture and form into small balls.

Bake: Arrange the balls on a greased baking sheet and bake for 30 minutes, or until firm.

Cool: Allow to cool before offering to your pet.

COD AND PEA PATTIES

Prep Time: 20 minutes | **Cook Time:** 10 minutes | **Total Time:** 30 minutes | **Yield:** 15 patties

Estimated calories per patty: 40 calories

Ingredients:
- 1/2 pound cod fillet, cooked and flaked
- 1 cup frozen peas, thawed
- 1 egg
- 1 cup breadcrumbs or oat flour

Instructions:

Prepare: Mash the peas in a bowl and mix with the flaked cod.

Bind: Stir in the egg and breadcrumbs or oat flour until you have a firm mixture.

Form Patties: Shape the mixture into small patties.

Cook: Pan-fry the patties in a lightly oiled skillet over medium heat for about 5 minutes on each side, or until golden and crispy.

Cool: Let the patties cool down to room temperature before serving to your dog.

FISH AND PUMPKIN CRACKERS

Prep Time: 15 minutes | **Cook Time:** 40 minutes | **Total Time:** 55 minutes | **Yield:** 30 crackers
Estimated calories per cracker: 20 calories
Ingredients:

- 1 cup canned fish (such as salmon or mackerel), drained
- 1/2 cup pumpkin puree
- 1 1/2 cups whole wheat flour (or substitute as needed)
- 1 egg

Instructions:
Preheat: Oven to 350°F (175°C). Line a baking sheet with parchment paper.
Mix: In a large bowl, combine the fish, pumpkin puree, flour, and egg. Stir until a stiff dough forms.
Roll Out: On a floured surface, roll the dough to about 1/4 inch thick. Use cookie cutters to cut into small cracker shapes.
Bake: Arrange crackers on the prepared baking sheet. Bake for 20 minutes, flip them, and then bake for another 20 minutes or until crisp.
Cool: Let the crackers cool before offering them to your dog as a crunchy treat.

SARDINE AND CARROT COOKIES

Prep Time: 10 minutes | **Cook Time:** 25 minutes | **Total Time:** 35 minutes | **Yield:** 2 dozen cookies
Estimated calories per cookie: 35 calories
Ingredients:

- 1 can sardines in water, drained and mashed
- 1 cup grated carrots
- 2 cups whole wheat flour
- 1/4 cup water

Instructions:
Preheat: Your oven to 350°F (175°C) and line a baking sheet with parchment paper.
Combine: Mix the mashed sardines, grated carrots, flour, and water in a bowl until a dough forms.
Shape: Take small spoonfuls of dough and form them into cookies. Place on the baking sheet.
Bake: For 25 minutes, or until the edges are golden brown.
Cool: Allow the cookies to cool completely before serving to your dog.

TUNA AND SWEET POTATO CUBES

Prep Time: 20 minutes | **Cook Time:** 1 hour to dehydrate | **Total Time:** 1 hour 20 minutes | **Yield:** Varies

Estimated calories per cube: 15 calories

Ingredients:
- 1 can tuna in water, drained
- 1 sweet potato, cooked and mashed
- 1 egg
- 1 cup oat flour

Instructions:

Preheat: Oven to 250°F (120°C) and line a baking sheet with parchment.
Mix: Combine tuna, mashed sweet potato, egg, and oat flour in a bowl until well mixed.
Shape: Press the mixture into a flat, even layer on the baking sheet, about 1/2 inch thick.
Cut: Use a knife or pizza cutter to score the mixture into small cubes.
Dehydrate: Bake for 1 hour, or until the cubes are dry and firm.
Cool: Break the cubes apart and let them cool before serving.

HERRING AND PEA PÂTÉ

Prep Time: 10 minutes | **Cook Time:** No cook | **Total Time:** 10 minutes | **Yield:** Varies

Estimated calories per serving: 25 calories

Ingredients:
- 1 can herring in water, drained
- 1/2 cup frozen peas, thawed
- 1 tablespoon plain Greek yogurt
- 2 tablespoons parsley, chopped

Instructions:

Blend: In a food processor, blend the herring, peas, Greek yogurt, and parsley until smooth.
Serve: This pâté can be served as is, or frozen in an ice cube tray for a cool treat.
Store: Keep the pâté in the fridge in an airtight container for up to 3 days.

SALMON AND SWEET POTATO DINNER

Prep Time: 15 minutes | **Cook Time**: 25 minutes | **Total Time**: 40 minutes | **Yield**: 4 servings
Estimated Calories per Serving: 300-350 calories
Ingredients:

- 1 pound fresh salmon fillet, skin removed and cubed
- 2 medium sweet potatoes, peeled and cubed
- 1 cup chopped green beans
- 1 tablespoon olive oil
- 2 tablespoons fish oil
- Water for steaming

Instructions:

Prep the vegetables: Steam the sweet potatoes and green beans until tender, about 10-15 minutes. Steaming helps preserve the nutrients and makes them easily digestible for dogs.
Cook the salmon: In a non-stick skillet, heat the olive oil over medium heat. Add the salmon cubes and cook until they are opaque and flaky, about 5-7 minutes, turning occasionally to ensure even cooking.
Combine and enrich: In a large bowl, combine the steamed sweet potatoes, green beans, and cooked salmon. Drizzle with the fish oil and gently mix to coat everything evenly.
Cool and serve: Allow the meal to cool to room temperature before serving to your dog.

SALMON AND PEA DINNER

Prep Time: 10 minutes | **Cook Time**: 20 minutes | **Total Time**: 30 minutes | **Yield**: 4 servings
Estimated Calories per Serving: 300-350 calories
Ingredients:

- 1 pound fresh salmon fillet, skin removed and cut into small pieces
- 1 cup frozen peas, thawed
- 1 cup cooked quinoa
- 1 tablespoon olive oil
- 2 cups low-sodium fish or vegetable broth

Instructions:

Cook the salmon: In a medium skillet, heat the olive oil over medium heat. Add the salmon pieces and sauté until the salmon is fully cooked and easily flakes with a fork, about 5-7 minutes.
Simmer with peas: Add the thawed peas to the skillet with the salmon, stir gently, and cook for an additional 2-3 minutes to warm the peas.
Prepare the quinoa: While the salmon cooks, prepare the quinoa according to the package instructions using water or broth for added flavor.
Combine ingredients: In a large bowl, mix the cooked salmon and peas with the quinoa. Ensure everything is evenly distributed.
Serve: Allow the meal to cool to room temperature before serving to your dog.

Vegetarian recipes

QUINOA VEGGIE PATTIES

Prep Time: 20 minutes | **Cook Time:** 30 minutes | **Total Time:** 50 minutes | **Yield:** 12 patties
Estimated calories per patty: 70 calories
Ingredients:
- 1 cup cooked quinoa
- 1/2 cup grated carrot
- 1/2 cup finely chopped spinach
- 1/4 cup applesauce
- 1/2 cup whole wheat flour
- 2 tablespoons ground flaxseed mixed with 6 tablespoons water (flax egg)

Instructions:
Preheat: Oven to 350°F (175°C) and line a baking sheet with parchment paper.
Combine: In a large bowl, mix together the cooked quinoa, grated carrot, spinach, applesauce, whole wheat flour, and flax egg until well combined.
Form Patties: Use your hands to form the mixture into patties and place them on the prepared baking sheet.
Bake: For 15 minutes, flip each patty, then bake for an additional 15 minutes or until the edges are golden brown.
Cool: Allow the patties to cool before serving to your dog.

SWEET POTATO AND LENTIL LOAF

Prep Time: 15 minutes | **Cook Time:** 1 hour | **Total Time:** 1 hour 15 minutes | **Yield:** 8 servings
Estimated calories per serving: 120 calories
Ingredients:
- 2 cups cooked and mashed sweet potato
- 1 cup cooked green lentils
- 1/2 cup peas
- 1/2 cup grated carrots
- 1 cup oat flour
- 1 teaspoon turmeric

Instructions:
Preheat: Oven to 375°F (190°C) and grease a loaf pan.
Mix: Combine all ingredients in a large bowl until thoroughly mixed.
Transfer: Spoon the mixture into the prepared loaf pan, pressing down to compact.
Bake: For 60 minutes, or until the loaf is firm and the top is slightly golden.
Cool: Let the loaf cool in the pan before slicing and serving to your dog.

VEGAN DOGGY COOKIES

Prep Time: 10 minutes | **Cook Time:** 25 minutes | **Total Time:** 35 minutes | **Yield:** 2 dozen cookies
Estimated calories per cookie: 50 calories
Ingredients:

- 2 bananas, mashed
- 1/4 cup unsweetened peanut butter (xylitol-free)
- 2 cups rolled oats
- 1/2 cup unsweetened applesauce
- 1 teaspoon cinnamon

Instructions:
Preheat: Oven to 350°F (175°C) and line a baking sheet with parchment paper.
Combine: In a large bowl, mix the mashed bananas, peanut butter, rolled oats, applesauce, and cinnamon until well blended.
Drop: Spoon drops of the mixture onto the prepared baking sheet, flattening each slightly with a fork.
Bake: For 25 minutes or until the edges are golden brown.
Cool: Allow the cookies to cool before serving.

PUMPKIN AND RICE BALLS

Prep Time: 20 minutes | **Cook Time:** No cook | **Total Time:** 20 minutes | **Yield:** 15 balls
Estimated calories per ball: 40 calories
Ingredients:

- 1 cup cooked brown rice, cooled
- 1/2 cup pumpkin puree
- 1/4 cup ground almonds
- 1/4 cup grated carrots
- 2 tablespoons parsley, finely chopped

Instructions:
Combine: In a medium bowl, mix together the brown rice, pumpkin puree, ground almonds, grated carrots, and parsley.
Form Balls: Roll the mixture into balls, using about a tablespoon of mixture per ball.
Chill: Place the balls in the refrigerator for at least an hour to set.
Serve: Offer the balls to your dog as a tasty vegetarian treat.

BROCCOLI AND CHICKPEA MASH

Prep Time: 10 minutes | **Cook Time:** 20 minutes | **Total Time:** 30 minutes | **Yield:** 4 servings

Estimated calories per serving: 100 calories

Ingredients:
- 1 cup chickpeas, cooked and drained
- 1 cup broccoli florets
- 1/4 cup nutritional yeast
- 1 tablespoon olive oil
- 1/2 teaspoon ground turmeric

Instructions:

Steam: Steam the broccoli until tender.

Mash: In a large bowl, combine the steamed broccoli, chickpeas, nutritional yeast, olive oil, and turmeric. Mash the ingredients together until you reach a consistent texture.

Serve: Allow the mash to cool to room temperature before serving to your dog.

GREEN VEGGIE AND BROWN RICE CASSEROLE

Prep Time: 10 minutes | **Cook Time:** 25 minutes | **Total Time**: 35 minutes | **Yield**: 4 servings

Estimated Calories per Serving: 200-250 calories

Ingredients:
- 1 cup brown rice
- 2 cups water
- 1 cup chopped broccoli
- 1/2 cup chopped zucchini
- 1/2 cup shredded carrots
- 1/4 cup chopped parsley
- 2 tablespoons coconut oil

Instructions:

Cook the rice: In a medium saucepan, combine the brown rice and water. Bring to a boil, then reduce the heat to low, cover, and simmer until the rice is fully cooked, about 20 minutes.

Steam the vegetables: While the rice is cooking, steam the broccoli, zucchini, and carrots until they are just tender, about 5-7 minutes.

Combine ingredients: In a large mixing bowl, combine the cooked rice, steamed vegetables, and chopped parsley. Stir in the coconut oil while the mixture is still warm to melt the oil and coat everything evenly.

Serve: Allow the casserole to cool to room temperature before serving to ensure it's safe for your dog.

Nutrient-rich recipes

CHICKEN AND VEGETABLE FLAXSEED DINNER

Prep Time: 15 minutes | **Cook Time**: 30 minutes | **Total Time**: 45 minutes | **Yield**: 4 servings
Estimated Calories per Serving: 250-300 calories
Ingredients:

- 1 pound boneless, skinless chicken breasts, cubed
- 1 cup brown rice
- 1 cup chopped carrots
- 1 cup chopped zucchini
- 1/4 cup ground flaxseeds
- 2 tablespoons olive oil
- 4 cups water or low-sodium chicken broth

Instructions:

Cook the rice: In a medium saucepan, cook the brown rice in water or broth according to package instructions. Typically, this involves bringing it to a boil, then covering and simmering until the rice is tender, about 20-25 minutes.

Cook the chicken: While the rice is cooking, heat olive oil in a large skillet over medium heat. Add the chicken cubes and cook until browned and no longer pink in the center, about 5-7 minutes.

Add vegetables: To the skillet with chicken, add the chopped carrots and zucchini. Cook for an additional 5-10 minutes, until the vegetables are tender.

Combine with flaxseeds: Once the chicken and vegetables are cooked, remove from heat and stir in the ground flaxseeds.

Mix with cooked rice: Combine the chicken and vegetable mixture with the cooked rice. Stir well to distribute all ingredients evenly.

Cool and serve: Allow the mixture to cool to room temperature before serving to your dog.

BALANCED BEEF STEW

Prep Time: 10 minutes | **Cook Time:** 2 hours | **Total Time:** 2 hours 10 minutes | **Yield:** 6 servings

Estimated calories per serving: 250 calories

Ingredients:
- 1 pound lean beef, cubed
- 1 sweet potato, cubed
- 1/2 cup carrots, diced
- 1/2 cup peas
- 1/2 cup green beans, chopped
- 4 cups low-sodium beef broth
- 2 tablespoons olive oil

Instructions:

Brown Beef: In a large pot, heat the olive oil over medium heat. Add the beef cubes and cook until all sides are browned.

Simmer: Add the sweet potato, carrots, peas, green beans, and beef broth to the pot. Bring to a boil, then reduce heat and simmer for about 2 hours, or until the beef is tender.

Cool: Let the stew cool completely before serving. This stew provides a balanced mix of protein, fiber, and essential vitamins.

CHICKEN AND RICE DINNER

Prep Time: 15 minutes | Cook Time: 45 minutes | **Total Time:** 1 hour | **Yield:** 4 servings

Estimated calories per serving: 300 calories

Ingredients:
- 2 chicken breasts, skinless and boneless
- 1 cup brown rice
- 1 cup spinach, chopped
- 1 apple, cored and cubed (ensure no seeds)
- 1 tablespoon coconut oil
- 4 cups water

Instructions:

Cook Chicken: In a pot, add the chicken breasts and water. Cook over medium heat for about 30 minutes, or until the chicken is fully cooked.

Cook Rice: In another pot, cook the brown rice as per the instructions on the package.

Combine: Once the chicken is cooked, shred it into small pieces. In a large bowl, mix the shredded chicken, cooked rice, spinach, and apple. Add coconut oil and mix well.

Serve: Allow the mixture to cool before serving. This meal is rich in protein, complex carbs, and vitamins.

OMEGA-3 FISH FEAST

Prep Time: 15 minutes | **Cook Time:** 20 minutes | **Total Time:** 35 minutes | **Yield:** 4 servings
Estimated calories per serving: 220 calories
Ingredients:

- 1 pound salmon, skin removed
- 1 cup quinoa
- 1/2 cup peas
- 1/2 cup carrots, finely chopped
- 3 cups water

Instructions:
Cook Quinoa: Rinse quinoa under cold water. In a pot, bring 2 cups of water to a boil. Add quinoa, reduce heat, cover, and simmer for about 15 minutes.
Steam Salmon: In a steamer over boiling water, steam the salmon for about 10 minutes, or until it flakes easily with a fork.
Steam Veggies: Steam the peas and carrots until tender.
Combine: Flake the salmon into small pieces and mix with the cooked quinoa and steamed vegetables.
Serve: Ensure the meal is at room temperature before serving. This dish is high in omega-3 fatty acids, essential for healthy skin and coat.

TURKEY AND VEGETABLE MASH

Prep Time: 10 minutes | **Cook Time:** 30 minutes | **Total Time:** 40 minutes | Yield: 4 servings
Estimated calories per serving: 280 calories
Ingredients:

- 1 pound ground turkey
- 1 cup cauliflower florets
- 1 cup broccoli florets
- 1/2 cup zucchini, chopped
- 2 tablespoons olive oil

Instructions:
Cook Turkey: In a skillet, heat the olive oil over medium heat. Add the ground turkey and cook until browned.
Steam Vegetables: Steam the cauliflower, broccoli, and zucchini until tender.
Mash: Combine the cooked turkey and steamed vegetables in a large bowl. Use a fork or potato masher to mash the ingredients together.
Serve: Once cooled, serve this nutrient-rich mash to your dog. This meal is packed with protein and essential vitamins from the vegetables.

VEGGIE-PACKED CANINE KIBBLE

Prep Time: 25 minutes | **Cook Time:** 40 minutes | **Total Time:** 1 hour 5 minutes | **Yield:** Varies
Estimated calories per serving: 300 calories (for a cup)
Ingredients:
- 2 cups chickpea flour
- 1 cup rolled oats
- 1/2 cup pumpkin puree
- 1/2 cup grated carrots
- 1/2 cup unsweetened applesauce
- 1/4 cup blueberries
- 2 tablespoons ground flaxseed
- 1 cup water

Instructions:
Preheat Oven: 350°F (175°C). Line a baking sheet with parchment paper.
Mix Dry Ingredients: In a large bowl, combine chickpea flour and rolled oats.
Add Wet Ingredients: Stir in pumpkin puree, grated carrots, applesauce, blueberries, and ground flaxseed. Gradually add water until the mixture forms a thick dough.
Form Kibble: Use a teaspoon to drop small, kibble-sized pieces onto the prepared baking sheet. Flatten slightly with the back of the spoon.
Bake: For 40 minutes, or until the kibble is dried and slightly golden.
Cool: Let the kibble cool completely before serving to your dog or storing in an airtight container.

PROTEIN POWER PUPSICLES

Prep Time: 10 minutes | **Freeze Time:** 4 hours | **Total Time:** 4 hours 10 minutes | **Yield:** 6 servings
Estimated calories per serving: 100 calories
Ingredients:
- 1 banana
- 1/2 cup peanut butter (xylitol-free)
- 1 cup plain Greek yogurt
- 1 tablespoon chia seeds

Instructions:
Blend: In a blender, combine the banana, peanut butter, Greek yogurt, and chia seeds until smooth.
Pour: Divide the mixture among popsicle molds or ice cube trays.
Freeze: Freeze for at least 4 hours, or until solid.
Serve: Run warm water over the outside of the molds to release the pupsicles before serving to your dog.

HEARTY BARLEY AND MUSHROOM STEW

Prep Time: 15 minutes | **Cook Time:** 1 hour | **Total Time:** 1 hour 15 minutes | **Yield:** 4 servings
Estimated calories per serving: 250 calories
Ingredients:

- 1 cup pearled barley, rinsed
- 1 cup chopped mushrooms
- 1 cup diced sweet potatoes
- 1/2 cup peas
- 4 cups low-sodium vegetable broth

Instructions:
Cook Barley: In a large pot, bring the vegetable broth to a boil. Add barley, reduce heat, cover, and simmer for 30 minutes.
Add Vegetables: Stir in mushrooms, sweet potatoes, and peas. Continue to simmer, covered, for an additional 30 minutes, or until the barley and vegetables are tender.
Cool: Allow the stew to cool before serving to your dog.

GREEN BEAN CRUNCHIES

Prep Time: 10 minutes | **Cook Time:** 25 minutes | **Total Time:** 35 minutes | **Yield:** Varies **Estimated calories per serving:** 10 calories per handful
Ingredients:

- 2 cups green beans, ends trimmed
- 1 tablespoon olive oil
- A pinch of turmeric (optional)

Instructions:
Preheat Oven: 400°F (200°C). Line a baking sheet with parchment paper.
Season: Toss the green beans with olive oil and turmeric until evenly coated.
Bake: Spread the green beans on the prepared baking sheet in a single layer. Bake for 25 minutes, or until crispy.
Cool: Let them cool before offering them as a crunchy, low-calorie treat.

BUTTERNUT SQUASH AND LENTIL LOAF

Prep Time: 20 minutes | **Cook Time:** 1 hour | **Total Time:** 1 hour 20 minutes | **Yield:** 6 servings

Estimated calories per serving: 180 calories

Ingredients:

- 1 cup red lentils, cooked and drained
- 2 cups butternut squash, cooked and mashed
- 1/2 cup rolled oats
- 2 tablespoons parsley, finely chopped
- 1 egg, beaten (optional, can use a flax egg for a vegan option)

Instructions:

Preheat Oven: 375°F (190°C). Grease a loaf pan.

Mix: In a large bowl, combine the lentils, butternut squash, rolled oats, parsley, and egg. Mix well until combined.

Bake: Press the mixture into the prepared loaf pan. Bake for 60 minutes, or until the top is browned and the loaf feels firm.

Cool: Let the loaf cool before slicing. Serve small portions as a nutrient-rich meal.

BEEF AND QUINOA DINNER

Prep Time: 15 minutes | **Cook Time**: 30 minutes | **Total Time**: 45 minutes | **Yield**: 4 servings

Estimated Calories per Serving: 300-350 calories

Ingredients:

- 1 pound lean ground beef
- 1 cup quinoa, rinsed
- 1/2 cup chopped kale
- 1/2 cup chopped carrots
- 1/4 cup blueberries
- 2 tablespoons flaxseed oil
- 3 cups water or low-sodium beef broth

Instructions:

Cook the quinoa: In a medium saucepan, combine the quinoa and water or broth. Bring to a boil, then cover, reduce heat to low, and simmer until quinoa is cooked and all liquid is absorbed, about 15-20 minutes.

Cook the beef: While the quinoa is cooking, heat a large skillet over medium heat. Add the ground beef and cook until browned and no longer pink, breaking it into small pieces as it cooks.

Steam vegetables: In a steamer or a pot with a small amount of water, steam the chopped kale and carrots until they are tender, about 5-7 minutes.

Combine ingredients: In a large bowl, mix the cooked quinoa, browned beef, steamed kale, carrots, and blueberries. Drizzle with flaxseed oil and stir to combine everything evenly.

Cool and serve: Allow the mixture to cool to room temperature before serving to ensure it's safe for your dog.

Seasonal recipes

SPRINGTIME CHICKEN AND ASPARAGUS MEAL

Prep Time: 15 minutes | **Cook Time:** 25 minutes | **Total Time:** 40 minutes | **Yield:** 4 servings
Estimated calories per serving: 250 calories
Ingredients:

- 1 pound chicken breast, cubed
- 1 cup asparagus, chopped into bite-size pieces
- 1 cup peas
- 1 sweet potato, cubed
- 2 tablespoons olive oil

Instructions:
Preheat Oven: 375°F (190°C).
Roast Sweet Potato: Toss sweet potato cubes with 1 tablespoon olive oil and spread on a baking sheet. Roast for 20 minutes or until tender.
Cook Chicken: In a skillet, heat the remaining olive oil over medium heat. Add chicken cubes and cook until no longer pink inside.
Steam Vegetables: Steam the asparagus and peas until tender, about 5-7 minutes.
Mix and Serve: Let all ingredients cool to room temperature. Combine chicken, sweet potato, asparagus, and peas in a bowl before serving to your dog.

SUMMERTIME BEEF AND ZUCCHINI SKEWERS

Prep Time: 20 minutes (plus marinating time) | **Cook Time:** 10 minutes | **Total Time:** 30 minutes + marinating | **Yield:** 6 skewers
Estimated calories per skewer: 180 calories
Ingredients:

- 1/2 pound lean beef, cut into 1-inch cubes
- 2 medium zucchinis, sliced into 1/2-inch rounds
- 1 bell pepper, cut into chunks
- Marinade: 1/4 cup apple cider vinegar, 2 tablespoons olive oil, 1 teaspoon dried oregano

Instructions:
Marinate Beef: Combine beef cubes with the marinade ingredients in a bowl. Cover and refrigerate for at least 2 hours.**Preheat Grill:** Medium-high heat.
Assemble Skewers: Thread marinated beef, zucchini slices, and bell pepper chunks onto skewers.
Grill: Cook skewers on the preheated grill, turning occasionally, until beef reaches desired doneness, about 10 minutes.
Cool and Serve: Allow skewers to cool (remove from skewers for smaller dogs) before serving.

AUTUMN PUMPKIN AND TURKEY STEW

Prep Time: 15 minutes | **Cook Time:** 1 hour | **Total Time:** 1 hour 15 minutes | **Yield:** 5 servings

Estimated calories per serving: 300 calories

Ingredients:
- 1 pound ground turkey
- 2 cups pumpkin puree (not pie filling)
- 1 apple, cored and cubed (ensure no seeds)
- 1/2 cup carrots, chopped
- 4 cups low-sodium chicken broth

Instructions:

Cook Turkey: In a large pot, brown the ground turkey over medium heat.

Add Ingredients: Add the pumpkin puree, apple cubes, carrots, and chicken broth to the pot.

Simmer: Bring to a boil, then reduce heat and simmer for about 45 minutes to an hour.

Cool: Allow the stew to cool before serving to your dog. This hearty stew is perfect for cooler autumn days.

WINTER WARM-UP SWEET POTATO AND LENTIL SOUP

Prep Time: 15 minutes | **Cook Time:** 45 minutes | **Total Time:** 1 hour | **Yield:** 4 servings

Estimated calories per serving: 200 calories

Ingredients:
- 1 cup lentils, rinsed
- 1 large sweet potato, peeled and cubed
- 1/2 cup celery, chopped
- 1/2 cup carrots, chopped
- 4 cups low-sodium vegetable broth

Instructions:

Simmer Lentils and Vegetables: In a large pot, combine lentils, sweet potato, celery, carrots, and vegetable broth. Bring to a boil, then reduce heat and simmer until lentils and sweet potatoes are tender, about 45 minutes.

Cool: Let the soup cool to room temperature before serving. This nutrient-rich soup is ideal for keeping your dog warm and satisfied during the winter months.

COOL CUCUMBER AND YOGURT SALAD FOR SUMMER

Prep Time: 10 minutes | Cook Time: 0 minutes | **Total Time:** 10 minutes | **Yield:** 3 servings
Estimated calories per serving: 100 calories
Ingredients:

- 1 large cucumber, diced
- 1/2 cup plain Greek yogurt
- 1 tablespoon fresh dill, chopped
- 1/4 cup watermelon, seedless and cubed (optional for extra hydration)

Instructions:
Combine Ingredients: In a large bowl, mix the diced cucumber, Greek yogurt, and fresh dill. If using, gently fold in the watermelon cubes.
Chill: Refrigerate the salad for about 30 minutes before serving to offer a refreshing and hydrating treat.
Serve: Ensure the salad is cool and serve a small portion to your dog as a delightful summer treat.

SPRING PEA AND CARROT RICE BOWL

Prep Time: 15 minutes | **Cook Time**: 30 minutes | **Total Time:** 45 minutes | **Yield:** 4 servings
Estimated calories per serving: 220 calories
Ingredients:

- 1 cup brown rice
- 2 cups water
- 1/2 pound lean chicken breast, cooked and shredded
- 1 cup fresh peas
- 1 cup carrots, diced
- 1 tablespoon olive oil

Instructions:
Cook Rice: In a medium pot, bring water to a boil. Add brown rice, reduce heat to low, cover, and simmer for about 45 minutes, or until water is absorbed and rice is tender.
Steam Vegetables: Steam peas and carrots until they are just tender, about 5-7 minutes.
Combine: In a large bowl, mix the cooked rice, steamed vegetables, and shredded chicken. Drizzle with olive oil and stir to combine.
Serve: Allow the mixture to cool before serving to your dog. This meal is perfect for spring when peas and carrots are at their peak.

SUMMER BERRY CHICKEN SALAD

Prep Time: 10 minutes | **Cook Time:** 0 minutes | **Total Time:** 10 minutes | **Yield:** 3 servings **Estimated calories per serving:** 200 calories

Ingredients:
- 1/2 pound cooked chicken breast, shredded
- 1/2 cup blueberries
- 1/2 cup sliced strawberries
- 1 cup spinach leaves, chopped
- 1 tablespoon flaxseed oil

Instructions:

Prepare Ingredients: Ensure all fruits and vegetables are washed thoroughly. Slice strawberries and chop spinach leaves.

Mix: In a large bowl, combine shredded chicken, blueberries, strawberries, and chopped spinach. Drizzle with flaxseed oil.

Serve: Toss gently to combine before serving. This refreshing salad is an excellent way to keep your dog hydrated and nourished during the hot summer months.

AUTUMN PUMPKIN BEEF MASH

Prep Time: 20 minutes | **Cook Time:** 1 hour | **Total Time:** 1 hour 20 minutes | **Yield:** 5 servings

Estimated calories per serving: 300 calories

Ingredients:
- 1 pound ground beef
- 2 cups pumpkin puree (not pie filling)
- 1 apple, cored and grated (ensure no seeds)
- 1/2 cup cranberries (fresh or unsweetened dried)
- 1 teaspoon cinnamon

Instructions:

Cook Beef: In a skillet over medium heat, cook the ground beef until browned. Drain any excess fat.

Mix: In a large bowl, combine the cooked beef, pumpkin puree, grated apple, cranberries, and cinnamon. Mix well.

Serve: Allow the mixture to cool to room temperature. This nutrient-rich mash celebrates the flavors of autumn and is packed with vitamins.

WINTER WARM BARLEY AND VEGGIE PORRIDGE

Prep Time: 10 minutes | **Cook Time:** 1 hour | **Total Time:** 1 hour 10 minutes | **Yield:** 4 servings
Estimated calories per serving: 250 calories
Ingredients:

- 1 cup pearled barley
- 4 cups low-sodium vegetable broth
- 1 cup chopped kale
- 1 cup diced butternut squash
- 1/2 cup diced carrots
- 2 tablespoons nutritional yeast

Instructions:
Cook Barley: In a large pot, bring the vegetable broth to a boil. Add barley, reduce heat, and simmer for about 30 minutes.
Add Vegetables: Add kale, butternut squash, and carrots to the pot. Continue to simmer until the vegetables are tender and barley is fully cooked, about 30 more minutes.
Finish: Stir in nutritional yeast for added flavor and nutrients.
Serve: Let the porridge cool to room temperature before serving. This hearty meal is perfect for keeping your dog warm and satisfied during the cold winter months.

SPRING HERB CHICKEN BAKE

Prep Time: 15 minutes | **Cook Time:** 25 minutes | **Total Time:** 40 minutes | **Yield:** 4 servings
Estimated calories per serving: 270 calories
Ingredients:

- 1/2 pound chicken breasts, cubed
- 1 cup new potatoes, quartered
- 1/2 cup fresh green beans, trimmed
- 1 tablespoon olive oil
- 1 teaspoon dried oregano
- 1 teaspoon dried parsley

Instructions:
Preheat Oven: 375°F (190°C).
Prepare Ingredients: Toss chicken, potatoes, and green beans with olive oil, oregano, and parsley in a large bowl.
Bake: Spread the mixture evenly on a baking sheet. Bake for 25 minutes, or until the chicken is cooked through and vegetables are tender.
Serve: Ensure the bake is cool before serving. This light yet satisfying dish is perfect for introducing the fresh flavors of spring to your dog's diet.

Sophisticated or Deluxe Options

LOBSTER AND SWEET PEA RISOTTO

Prep Time: 20 minutes | **Cook Time:** 45 minutes | **Total Time:** 1 hour 5 minutes | **Yield:** 4 servings
Estimated calories per serving: 350 calories

Ingredients:
- 1 small lobster tail, cooked and meat removed (about 1/2 cup lobster meat)
- 1 cup arborio rice
- 2 cups low-sodium chicken or vegetable broth, warmed
- 1/2 cup fresh sweet peas
- 1/4 cup finely grated carrots
- 1 tablespoon olive oil
- A pinch of finely chopped parsley for garnish

Instructions:
Prepare Risotto: In a large skillet, heat olive oil over medium heat. Add arborio rice and toast lightly for 2 minutes, stirring constantly.
Add Broth: Gradually add warm broth, one ladle at a time, allowing the rice to absorb the liquid before adding more. Stir continuously.
Combine: Once the rice is tender and creamy (about 30 minutes), stir in the lobster meat, sweet peas, and grated carrots. Cook for an additional 5 minutes.
Garnish and Serve: Garnish with parsley. Allow cooling to a safe temperature before serving to your dog. This luxurious meal provides a rich source of protein and fiber.

QUAIL EGG AND SPINACH OMELETTE

Prep Time: 10 minutes | **Cook Time:** 10 minutes | **Total Time:** 20 minutes | **Yield:** 2 servings
Estimated calories per serving: 180 calories

Ingredients:
- 4 quail eggs, beaten
- 1/2 cup chopped spinach
- 1/4 cup finely diced cooked chicken breast
- 1 teaspoon coconut oil

Instructions:
Cook Spinach: In a non-stick skillet, heat coconut oil over medium heat. Add spinach and sauté until wilted, about 2 minutes.
Add Eggs and Chicken: Pour the beaten quail eggs over the spinach. Sprinkle the diced chicken evenly across the egg mixture.
Cook Omelette: Let the eggs set at the bottom, then gently fold the omelette in half. Cook until the eggs are fully set but still moist.
Cool and Serve: Allow the omelette to cool and cut it into manageable pieces for your dog. This protein-rich omelette is perfect for a sophisticated brunch or dinner treat.

SEARED DUCK WITH BLUEBERRY COMPOTE

Prep Time: 15 minutes | **Cook Time:** 25 minutes | **Total Time:** 40 minutes | **Yield:** 3 servings
Estimated calories per serving: 400 calories

Ingredients:

- 1 duck breast, skin removed
- 1 cup fresh blueberries
- 1 teaspoon honey (optional, omit if your dog is sensitive to sugars)
- 1/2 cup water
- 1 tablespoon olive oil

Instructions:

Seared Duck: Heat olive oil in a skillet over medium-high heat. Add the duck breast and sear on both sides until browned and cooked through, about 5-7 minutes per side. Let it cool, then slice thinly.

Blueberry Compote: In a small saucepan, combine blueberries, water, and honey (if using). Simmer over low heat until the berries have softened and the mixture has thickened, about 15 minutes.

Combine: Spoon the blueberry compote over the sliced duck.

Serve: Allow the dish to cool before serving. This deluxe meal combines rich, lean protein from the duck with antioxidants from the blueberries, making it a nutrient-packed choice for your dog.

GOURMET TURKEY AND CRANBERRY DOG FEAST

Prep Time: 20 minutes | **Cook Time:** 40 minutes | **Total Time:** 1 hour | **Yield:** 4 servings
Estimated Calories per Serving: 350-400 calories

Ingredients:

- 1 pound ground turkey
- 1/2 cup fresh cranberries (or unsweetened dried cranberries if fresh aren't available)
- 1 sweet potato, peeled and diced
- 1/2 cup green beans, chopped
- 1/4 cup carrots, diced
- 1 cup brown rice
- 1 tablespoon olive oil
- 2 cups low-sodium chicken or turkey broth

Instructions:

Cook the rice: In a saucepan, bring the brown rice and broth to a boil. Reduce heat to low, cover, and simmer until the rice is tender, about 30-40 minutes.

Prepare the vegetables and turkey: In another pan, heat the olive oil over medium heat. Add the ground turkey and cook until browned. Add the sweet potato, carrots, and green beans. Cook until the vegetables are just tender, about 10 minutes.

Add cranberries: Stir in the cranberries and cook for another 5 minutes until they are slightly softened.

Combine with rice: Mix the cooked rice and turkey-vegetable mixture together.

Cool and serve: Allow the feast to cool to room temperature before serving to your dog.

SALMON AND DILL DELICACY

Prep Time: 15 minutes | **Cook Time**: 20 minutes | **Total Time**: 35 minutes | **Yield**: 4 servings

Estimated Calories per Serving: 300-350 calories

Ingredients:
- 1 pound salmon fillet, skin removed
- 1/4 cup finely chopped dill
- 1/2 cup quinoa
- 1/4 cup peas
- 1/4 cup chopped carrots
- 1 tablespoon coconut oil
- 2 cups water

Instructions:

Cook the quinoa: In a saucepan, combine the quinoa with water. Bring to a boil, then cover and simmer until the quinoa is fluffy and the water is absorbed, about 15 minutes.

Prepare the salmon: In a skillet, heat the coconut oil over medium heat. Add the salmon and cook until it flakes easily with a fork, about 5-7 minutes per side.

Steam vegetables: In a steamer, steam the peas and carrots until tender, about 5-7 minutes.

Flake the salmon and combine: Once cooked, flake the salmon into small pieces. In a large bowl, mix the flaked salmon, cooked quinoa, steamed vegetables, and chopped dill.

Cool and serve: Allow the dish to cool before serving to ensure it's at a safe temperature for your dog.

BEEF AND BLUEBERRY BLISS

Prep Time: 15 minutes | **Cook Time**: 25 minutes | **Total Time**: 40 minutes | **Yield**: 4 servings

Estimated Calories per Serving: 300-350 calories

Ingredients:
- 1 pound lean ground beef
- 1/2 cup blueberries
- 1/2 cup chopped spinach
- 1/2 cup cooked millet
- 1/4 cup chopped carrots
- 1 tablespoon flaxseed oil
- 2 cups water or low-sodium beef broth

Instructions:

Cook the millet: In a saucepan, simmer the millet in water or broth until all liquid is absorbed and millet is tender, about 15-20 minutes.

Cook the beef: In a skillet, cook the ground beef over medium heat until browned and no longer pink, breaking it into small pieces as it cooks, about 8-10 minutes.

Steam vegetables: Steam the carrots and spinach until tender, about 5-7 minutes.

Combine all ingredients: In a large bowl, mix the cooked millet, beef, steamed vegetables, and blueberries. Drizzle with flaxseed oil and stir to combine thoroughly.

Cool and serve: To make it safe for the dog, let the mixture cool to room temperature before serving.

Sensitive Stomach Options

GENTLE CHICKEN AND RICE

Prep Time: 10 minutes | **Cook Time:** 20 minutes | **Total Time:** 30 minutes | **Yield:** 4 servings
Estimated calories per serving: 200 calories
Ingredients:

- 1 cup boiled chicken breast, shredded (no skin or bones)
- 1 cup cooked white rice
- 1/2 cup plain pumpkin puree (not pie filling)
- A pinch of parsley (optional, for flavor)

Instructions:

Boil Chicken: Boil the chicken breast until fully cooked, then let it cool and shred it, ensuring there are no bones or skin.
Cook Rice: Cook white rice according to package instructions until soft.
Mix: In a large bowl, combine the shredded chicken, cooked rice, and pumpkin puree. Add a pinch of parsley if desired.
Serve: Allow the mixture to cool to room temperature before serving to your dog. This simple recipe is easy on the stomach and ideal for dogs needing a bland diet.

SENSITIVE STOMACH FISH PATTIES

Prep Time: 15 minutes | **Cook Time:** 15 minutes | **Total Time:** 30 minutes | **Yield:** 6 patties
Estimated calories per patty: 150 calories
Ingredients:

- 1/2 pound white fish (e.g., cod or tilapia), cooked and flaked
- 1/2 cup cooked quinoa
- 1 egg, beaten
- 1 tablespoon finely chopped parsley
- Coconut oil (for cooking)

Instructions:

Preheat Pan: Lightly grease a skillet with coconut oil and heat over medium heat.
Combine Ingredients: In a large bowl, mix the flaked fish, cooked quinoa, beaten egg, and parsley until well combined.
Form Patties: Shape the mixture into small patties.
Cook: Fry each patty in the skillet for about 3-4 minutes on each side or until golden brown and cooked through.
Cool: Let the patties cool before serving. These patties are rich in omega-3 fatty acids, which can help soothe inflammation in sensitive stomachs.

TURKEY AND SWEET POTATO MASH

Prep Time: 15 minutes | **Cook Time:** 30 minutes | **Total Time:** 45 minutes | **Yield:** 4 servings

Estimated calories per serving: 250 calories

Ingredients:
- 1 pound ground turkey, cooked and drained
- 2 medium sweet potatoes, boiled and mashed
- 1/4 cup low-sodium chicken broth (ensure it's onion-free)
- 1 tablespoon olive oil

Instructions:

Cook Turkey: Cook the ground turkey in a skillet over medium heat until browned. Drain any excess fat.

Mash Sweet Potatoes: Peel the boiled sweet potatoes and mash them until smooth.

Mix: Combine the cooked turkey, mashed sweet potatoes, and chicken broth in a large bowl. Stir in olive oil to add healthy fats.

Serve: Once cooled, this mash provides a nutrient-dense meal that's gentle on your dog's stomach.

DIGESTIVE SOOTHING OATMEAL

Prep Time: 5 minutes | **Cook Time:** 10 minutes | **Total Time:** 15 minutes | **Yield:** 2 servings

Estimated calories per serving: 100 calories

Ingredients:
- 1 cup rolled oats
- 2 cups water
- 1/2 apple, grated (ensure no seeds)
- 1 tablespoon plain, unsweetened yogurt

Instructions:

Cook Oatmeal: In a pot, bring water to a boil. Add rolled oats and simmer for about 10 minutes, or until the oats are soft.

Add Apple: Stir in the grated apple into the cooked oatmeal.

Cool and Add Yogurt: Allow the oatmeal to cool to room temperature, then stir in the plain yogurt.

Serve: This oatmeal is soothing for the digestive tract and includes probiotics from yogurt to support gut health.

GENTLE DIGEST LAMB AND PARSNIP PUREE

Prep Time: 15 minutes | **Cook Time:** 25 minutes | **Total Time:** 40 minutes | **Yield:** 4 servings
Estimated calories per serving: 220 calories

Ingredients:

- 1/2 pound ground lamb (lean, cooked, and drained)
- 2 medium parsnips, peeled and cubed
- 1 small sweet potato, peeled and cubed
- 1/4 cup plain, unsweetened applesauce
- 2 tablespoons olive oil

Instructions:

Cook Vegetables: In a pot, boil parsnips and sweet potato until tender, about 20 minutes.
Puree: Drain the vegetables and allow them to cool. Blend the parsnips, sweet potato, and applesauce in a food processor until smooth.
Mix with Lamb: Stir the puree into the cooked ground lamb until evenly mixed. Drizzle with olive oil to incorporate healthy fats.
Serve: Allow the puree to cool to room temperature before serving. This puree offers a mix of protein and vitamins while being gentle on the stomach.

SOOTHING CHICKEN BROTH BOWL

Prep Time: 10 minutes | **Cook Time:** 1 hour | **Total Time:** 1 hour 10 minutes | **Yield:** 4 servings
Estimated calories per serving: 150 calories

Ingredients:

- 1 chicken breast (boneless, skinless)
- 1/2 cup rice, rinsed
- 1 carrot, peeled and finely diced
- 4 cups water or low-sodium, onion-free chicken broth
- A few parsley leaves for garnish

Instructions:

Simmer Chicken and Rice: In a large pot, add chicken breast, rice, carrot, and water or broth. Bring to a boil, then reduce heat and simmer for about 1 hour, or until the chicken is tender and the rice is cooked.
Shred Chicken: Remove the chicken, let it cool, then shred it into small, manageable pieces for your dog.
Combine: Add the shredded chicken back into the pot with rice and carrots. Stir well.
Garnish: Sprinkle a few parsley leaves on top before serving. This broth bowl is hydrating and easy on the digestive system, with the added benefit of nutrients from the carrot.

HYPOALLERGENIC FISH FLAKES

Prep Time: 15 minutes | **Cook Time:** 20 minutes | **Total Time:** 35 minutes | **Yield:** 3 servings

Estimated calories per serving: 180 calories

Ingredients:
- 1/2 pound white fish (such as cod or tilapia), deboned
- 1 cup cooked pumpkin, mashed
- 1/2 cup cooked peas
- 1 tablespoon coconut oil

Instructions:

Cook Fish: Steam or bake the fish until it flakes easily with a fork. Let it cool, then flake the fish into small, bite-sized pieces.

Mix Ingredients: In a bowl, gently mix the fish flakes, mashed pumpkin, and peas. Drizzle with melted coconut oil for additional healthy fats.

Serve: Ensure the mixture is at room temperature before serving. This meal is rich in omega-3 fatty acids and gentle on the stomach, making it ideal for dogs with food sensitivities.

FISH AND SWEET POTATO DIGESTIVE HEALTH MEAL

Prep Time: 15 minutes | **Cook Time:** 30 minutes | **Total Time:** 45 minutes | **Yield**: 4 servings

Estimated Calories per Serving: 250-300 calories

Ingredients:
- 1 pound white fish fillets (e.g., cod, tilapia), chopped into small, bite-sized pieces
- 2 medium sweet potatoes, peeled and cubed
- 1/2 cup chopped green beans
- 1 tablespoon olive oil
- 2 cups low-sodium fish or vegetable broth

Instructions:

Cook sweet potatoes: In a medium pot, bring the sweet potatoes and broth to a boil. Reduce heat and simmer until the potatoes begin to soften, about 15 minutes.

Add fish and beans: Add the chopped fish and green beans to the pot. Continue to simmer until the fish is cooked through and the beans are tender, about 10-15 minutes. The fish should be easily flaked with a fork.

Cool and serve: Allow the meal to cool to room temperature before serving to ensure it's safe for your dog.

Special Diet Options

LOW-FAT CHICKEN AND VEGETABLE STEW FOR WEIGHT MANAGEMENT

Prep Time: 15 minutes | **Cook Time:** 1 hour | **Total Time:** 1 hour 15 minutes | **Yield:** 5 servings
Estimated calories per serving: 200 calories

Ingredients:
- 1 pound skinless chicken breast, cubed
- 2 carrots, peeled and diced
- 1 zucchini, diced
- 1 cup green beans, chopped
- 4 cups low-sodium chicken broth
- 1 tablespoon olive oil

Instructions:

Cook Chicken: In a large pot, heat the olive oil over medium heat. Add the chicken cubes and cook until no longer pink.

Add Vegetables and Broth: Add carrots, zucchini, and green beans to the pot. Pour in the chicken broth.

Simmer: Bring to a boil, then reduce heat and simmer for about 45 minutes, or until vegetables are tender.

Serve: Allow the stew to cool to room temperature. This low-fat stew helps manage weight while providing essential nutrients.

HYPOALLERGENIC FISH AND SWEET POTATO MASH FOR ALLERGIES

Prep Time: 20 minutes | **Cook Time:** 30 minutes | **Total Time:** 50 minutes | **Yield:** 4 servings
Estimated calories per serving: 220 calories

Ingredients:
- 1/2 pound salmon, skin removed
- 2 medium sweet potatoes, peeled and cubed
- 1 tablespoon coconut oil
- 1/2 cup peas (optional, check for allergies)

Instructions:

Cook Sweet Potato: Boil sweet potatoes until tender, then mash.

Bake Salmon: Preheat oven to 375°F (190°C). Place salmon on a baking sheet, brush with coconut oil, and bake for 20 minutes.

Combine: Flake the cooked salmon into the mashed sweet potato. Stir in peas if using.

Serve: Cool to room temperature. This hypoallergenic recipe is gentle for dogs with sensitive systems or specific protein allergies.

HIGH-FIBER BEEF AND PUMPKIN RECIPE FOR DIGESTIVE HEALTH

Prep Time: 15 minutes | **Cook Time:** 1 hour | **Total Time:** 1 hour 15 minutes | **Yield:** 4 servings

Estimated calories per serving: 250 calories

Ingredients:

- 1 pound lean ground beef
- 2 cups pumpkin puree (not pie filling)
- 1/2 cup brown rice, cooked
- 1 carrot, shredded
- 1/4 cup ground flaxseed

Instructions:

Cook Beef: Brown the ground beef in a skillet over medium heat, then drain any excess fat.

Mix Ingredients: In a large bowl, combine the cooked beef, pumpkin puree, cooked brown rice, shredded carrot, and ground flaxseed.

Serve: Ensure the mixture is cool. This high-fiber meal supports digestive health and regular bowel movements.

KIDNEY CARE RECIPE WITH LOW PHOSPHORUS

Prep Time: 20 minutes | **Cook Time:** 40 minutes | **Total Time:** 1 hour | **Yield:** 4 servings

Estimated calories per serving: 180 calories

Ingredients:

- 1/2 pound ground turkey, cooked and drained
- 1 cup cooked cauliflower, mashed
- 1/4 cup cooked egg whites, chopped
- 1/8 cup carrots, boiled and mashed
- 2 tablespoons olive oil

Instructions:

Prepare Ingredients: Ensure all ingredients are cooked as specified and at room temperature.

Mix: In a bowl, gently mix the ground turkey, mashed cauliflower, chopped egg whites, and mashed carrots. Drizzle with olive oil to enhance palatability and add healthy fats.

Serve: This low-phosphorus meal is suitable for dogs with kidney issues, helping to manage their condition while providing necessary nutrition.

LOW-SODIUM CHICKEN SOUP FOR HEART HEALTH

Prep Time: 15 minutes | **Cook Time:** 1 hour | **Total Time:** 1 hour 15 minutes | **Yield:** 4 servings
Estimated calories per serving: 180 calories

- **Ingredients:**
- 1 pound skinless chicken breasts
- 4 cups water
- 1 cup sliced carrots
- 1 cup chopped green beans
- 1/2 cup chopped celery
- 1 tablespoon fresh parsley, finely chopped

Instructions:

Prepare Chicken: Place chicken breasts in a large pot and cover with water. Bring to a boil, then simmer for about 30 minutes until the chicken is fully cooked.

Add Vegetables: Add carrots, green beans, and celery to the pot. Continue to simmer for another 20-30 minutes until the vegetables are tender.

Shred Chicken: Remove the chicken, shred it into bite-sized pieces, and return it to the pot. Stir in fresh parsley.

Serve: Cool the soup to room temperature before serving. This low-sodium soup supports heart health and is gentle on the digestive system.

GRAIN-FREE TURKEY AND VEGETABLE PATTIES FOR DOGS WITH GRAIN ALLERGIES

Prep Time: 20 minutes | **Cook Time:** 35 minutes | **Total Time:** 55 minutes | **Yield:** 6 patties
Estimated calories per patty: 220 calories

Ingredients:

- 1/2 pound ground turkey
- 1/4 cup grated zucchini
- 1/4 cup grated sweet potato
- 2 tablespoons coconut flour
- 1 egg, beaten

Instructions:

Preheat Oven: 375°F (190°C). Line a baking tray with parchment paper.

Combine Ingredients: In a large bowl, mix together the ground turkey, grated zucchini, sweet potato, coconut flour, and egg until well combined.

Form Patties: Shape the mixture into patties and place them on the prepared baking tray.

Bake: For about 35 minutes, or until the patties are cooked through and slightly golden on the outside.

Cool: Allow the patties to cool before serving. These grain-free patties are perfect for dogs with grain sensitivities or allergies.

ANTIOXIDANT-RICH BLUEBERRY AND SPINACH PUREE FOR IMMUNE SUPPORT

Prep Time: 10 minutes | **Cook Time:** 0 minutes | **Total Time:** 10 minutes | **Yield:** 3 servings

Estimated calories per serving: 100 calories

Ingredients:
- 1 cup fresh blueberries
- 1 cup fresh spinach leaves
- 1/2 banana
- 1/4 cup plain, unsweetened yogurt

Instructions:

Blend: In a blender, combine blueberries, spinach, banana, and yogurt. Blend until smooth.

Serve: Offer the puree as a special treat or mix it with your dog's regular food for an antioxidant boost.

Store: Any leftovers can be stored in the refrigerator for up to 2 days.

OMEGA-3 RICH SALMON AND QUINOA DINNER FOR SKIN AND COAT HEALTH

Prep Time: 15 minutes | **Cook Time:** 20 minutes | **Total Time:** 35 minutes | **Yield:** 4 servings

Estimated calories per serving: 300 calories

Ingredients:
- 1/2 pound salmon fillet, cooked and flaked
- 1 cup cooked quinoa
- 1/2 cup chopped kale
- 2 tablespoons olive oil
- 1 tablespoon ground flaxseed

Instructions:

Prepare Ingredients: Ensure the salmon is cooked thoroughly, then flake it. Cook quinoa according to package instructions. Steam kale until tender.

Combine: In a bowl, mix the flaked salmon, cooked quinoa, and kale. Add olive oil and ground flaxseed for an omega-3 boost.

Serve: Once the mixture has cooled to room temperature, it's ready to be served. This meal is particularly beneficial for improving skin and coat health due to its high omega-3 content.

Fresh, Uncooked Foods

BASIC RAW BEEF DINNER

Prep Time: 10 minutes | **Total Time:** 10 minutes | **Yield:** 2 servings
Estimated calories per serving: 250 calories
Ingredients:

- 1/2 pound lean ground beef (make sure it's fresh and from a reliable source)
- 1/4 cup raw liver, finely chopped
- 1/4 cup grated carrots
- 2 tablespoons pureed pumpkin (not pie filling)
- 1 tablespoon ground flaxseed

Instructions:

Mix: In a large bowl, combine the ground beef, raw liver, grated carrots, pureed pumpkin, and ground flaxseed.
Serve: Divide the mixture into two portions. Serve one portion to your dog and store the other in the refrigerator for the next meal.

CHICKEN AND APPLE RAW MEAL

Prep Time: 10 minutes | **Total Time:** 10 minutes | **Yield:** 2 servings
Estimated calories per serving: 200 calories
Ingredients:

- 1/2 pound chicken breast, chopped into small, bite-sized pieces
- 1/4 cup finely chopped raw spinach
- 1/4 apple, grated (ensure no seeds)
- 1 tablespoon olive oil
- 2 tablespoons plain yogurt

Instructions:

Combine: In a bowl, mix together the chicken pieces, chopped spinach, grated apple, olive oil, and yogurt until well blended.
Serve: Immediately offer one portion to your dog. Refrigerate the remaining portion for later.

TURKEY AND CRANBERRY FESTIVE MIX

Prep Time: 15 minutes | **Total Time:** 15 minutes | **Yield:** 3 servings

Estimated calories per serving: 230 calories

Ingredients:

- 1/2 pound ground turkey (choose human-grade, lean meat)
- 1/4 cup raw cranberries, finely chopped (ensure they are unsweetened and not dried)
- 1/4 cup diced celery
- 1/4 cup pumpkin seeds, ground
- 1 egg, beaten (optional, use only if your dog is used to consuming raw eggs)

Instructions:

Prepare: In a mixing bowl, thoroughly combine the ground turkey, cranberries, celery, ground pumpkin seeds, and the beaten egg (if using).

Portion: Divide the mixture into three equal portions. Serve one portion to your dog and store the rest in the refrigerator.

SALMON AND VEGGIE RAW BLEND

Prep Time: 10 minutes | **Total Time:** 10 minutes | **Yield:** 2 servings

Estimated calories per serving: 300 calories

Ingredients:

- 1/2 pound salmon fillet, skin removed and chopped into small pieces
- 1/4 cup chopped kale
- 1/4 cup shredded zucchini
- 1 tablespoon coconut oil
- 1 teaspoon seaweed powder

Instructions:

Mix: In a large bowl, gently mix the chopped salmon, kale, zucchini, coconut oil, and seaweed powder.

Serve: Offer half of the mixture to your dog, ensuring it's at a safe, room temperature. Store the remaining half in the refrigerator for the next meal.

RAW LAMB AND MINT MIX

Prep Time: 10 minutes | **Total Time:** 10 minutes | **Yield:** 2 servings

Estimated calories per serving: 300 calories

Ingredients:

- 1/2 pound ground lamb (choose fresh, high-quality meat)
- 1/4 cup fresh mint leaves, finely chopped
- 1/4 cup grated carrots
- 1/4 cup finely chopped kale
- 2 tablespoons blueberries

Instructions:

Prepare: In a mixing bowl, combine the ground lamb, mint leaves, grated carrots, chopped kale, and blueberries. Mix until evenly distributed.

Serve: Divide the mixture into two equal portions. Offer one to your dog and store the remaining portion in the refrigerator for later.

BEEFY BLUEBERRY BLEND

Prep Time: 10 minutes | **Total Time:** 10 minutes | **Yield:** 3 servings

Estimated calories per serving: 280 calories

Ingredients:

- 1/2 pound lean ground beef
- 1/4 cup raw beef liver, finely chopped
- 1/2 cup blueberries
- 1/4 cup shredded zucchini
- 1 tablespoon ground flaxseeds

Instructions:

Combine: In a large bowl, thoroughly mix the ground beef, beef liver, blueberries, shredded zucchini, and ground flaxseeds.

Portion: Create three equally sized portions. Serve one immediately and refrigerate the others for future meals.

RAW TURKEY AND CRANBERRY DELIGHT

Prep Time: 15 minutes | **Total Time:** 15 minutes | **Yield:** 4 servings

Estimated calories per serving: 250 calories

Ingredients:
- 1/2 pound ground turkey
- 1/4 cup cranberries, finely chopped (ensure they're fresh and unsweetened)
- 1/4 cup diced cucumber
- 1/4 cup pumpkin puree
- 1 egg yolk (optional, ensure your dog tolerates raw egg)

Instructions:

Mix: Blend the ground turkey, cranberries, cucumber, pumpkin puree, and egg yolk (if using) in a large bowl until well combined.

Serve: Divide the mixture into four servings, offering one to your dog and storing the rest in the refrigerator.

FISH AND VEGGIE RAW FEAST

Prep Time: 10 minutes | **Total Time:** 10 minutes | **Yield:** 2 servings

Estimated calories per serving: 320 calories

Ingredients:
- 1/2 pound skinless mackerel or sardines, chopped
- 1/4 cup finely chopped spinach
- 1/4 cup finely diced sweet potato (raw)
- 2 tablespoons chopped parsley
- 1 tablespoon hemp seeds

Instructions:

Prepare: Thoroughly mix the chopped fish, spinach, sweet potato, parsley, and hemp seeds in a bowl until the ingredients are evenly distributed.

Serve: Divide the mixture into two portions, offering one to your dog and refrigerating the remainder.

Part 3: 30-Day Meal Plan

Meal Plan for Your Dog

Day 1:
Breakfast: Chicken and Vegetable Flaxseed Dinner
Dinner: Salmon and Sweet Potato Dinner
Treat: Carrot and Apple Treats
Day 2:
Breakfast: Beef and Sweet Potato Soup
Dinner: Quinoa Veggie Patties
Treat: Sweet Potato Chewies
Day 3:
Breakfast: Balanced Beef Stew
Dinner: Turkey and Rice Comfort Soup
Treat: Spinach, Carrot, and Zucchini Dog Treats
Day 4:
Breakfast: Chicken and Rice Dinner
Dinner: Veggie-Packed Canine Kibble
Treat: Frozen Yogurt Pops
Day 5:
Breakfast: Omega-3 Fish Feast
Dinner: Veggie Broth Delight
Treat: Beef and Veggie Balls
Day 6:
Breakfast: Turkey and Vegetable Mash
Dinner: Lamb and Mint Soup
Treat: Turkey and Sweet Potato Meatballs
Day 7:
Breakfast: Hearty Barley and Mushroom Stew
Dinner: Duck and Pear Puree
Treat: Apple Cinnamon Dog Cookies
Day 8:
Breakfast: Salmon and Sweet Potato Jerky
Dinner: Quinoa Vegetable Stew
Treat: Salmon and Sweet Pea Treats

Day 9:
Breakfast: Tuna and Parsley Biscuits
Dinner: Sweet Potato and Lentil Loaf
Treat: Beefy Squash Bites
Day 10:
Breakfast: Shrimp and Rice Balls
Dinner: Vegan Doggy Cookies
Treat: Cheesy Veggie Muffins
Day 11:
Breakfast: Cod and Pea Patties
Dinner: Pumpkin and Rice Balls
Treat: Apple and Oatmeal Dog Snacks
Day 12:
Breakfast: Sardine and Carrot Cookies
Dinner: Butternut Squash and Lentil Loaf
Treat: Sweet Potato Fries for Dogs
Day 13:
Breakfast: Tuna and Sweet Potato Cubes
Dinner: Broccoli and Chickpea Mash
Treat: Peanut Butter and Pumpkin Dog Treats
Day 14:
Breakfast: Herring and Pea Pâté
Dinner: Green Bean Crunchies
Treat: Chicken and Rice Dog Biscuits
Day 15:
Breakfast: Chicken and Barley Broth
Dinner: Protein Power Pupsicles
Treat: Beefy Veggie Soup
Day 16:
Breakfast: Beefy Veggie Soup
Dinner: Quinoa Veggie Patties
Treat: Frozen Yogurt Pops

Day 17:
Breakfast: Fish and Pumpkin Crackers
Dinner: Chicken and Pumpkin Broth
Treat: Turkey and Sweet Potato Meatballs
Day 18:
Breakfast: Lamb and Mint Soup
Dinner: Sweet Potato and Lentil Loaf
Treat: Apple Cinnamon Dog Cookies
Day 19:
Breakfast: Quinoa Vegetable Stew
Dinner: Beef and Sweet Potato Soup
Treat: Salmon and Sweet Pea Treats
Day 20:
Breakfast: Duck and Pear Puree
Dinner: Vegan Doggy Cookies
Treat: Cheesy Veggie Muffins
Day 21:
Breakfast: Omega-3 Fish Feast
Dinner: Chicken and Vegetable Flaxseed Dinner
Treat: Beefy Squash Bites
Day 22:
Breakfast: Turkey and Vegetable Mash
Dinner: Veggie-Packed Canine Kibble
Treat: Peanut Butter and Pumpkin Dog Treats
Day 23:
Breakfast: Balanced Beef Stew
Dinner: Hearty Barley and Mushroom Stew
Treat: Apple and Oatmeal Dog Snacks

Day 24:
Breakfast: Chicken and Rice Dinner
Dinner: Lamb and Mint Soup
Treat: Turkey and Sweet Potato Meatballs
Day 25:
Breakfast: Salmon and Sweet Potato Dinner
Dinner: Beefy Veggie Soup
Treat: Frozen Yogurt Pops
Day 26:
Breakfast: Veggie Broth Delight
Dinner: Quinoa Vegetable Stew
Treat: Sweet Potato Fries for Dogs
Day 27:
Breakfast: Duck and Pear Puree
Dinner: Vegan Doggy Cookies
Treat: Beef and Veggie Balls
Day 28:
Breakfast: Salmon and Sweet Potato Jerky
Dinner: Sweet Potato and Lentil Loaf
Treat: Apple Cinnamon Dog Cookies
Day 29:
Breakfast: Tuna and Parsley Biscuits
Dinner: Green Bean Crunchies
Treat: Salmon and Sweet Pea Treats
Day 30:
Breakfast: Shrimp and Rice Balls
Dinner: Protein Power Pupsicles
Treat: Cheesy Veggie Muffins

CONCLUSION

As we close the pages of this cookbook, you're now equipped not just with a collection of recipes, but with a new perspective on what it means to nourish your beloved dog.

Remember, each meal you prepare is a step toward a healthier, happier life for your furry companion. The knowledge and tips shared throughout this book aim to empower you as a pet owner to make the best dietary choices for your dog's individual needs.

From understanding the basics of dog nutrition to mastering the art of creating tasty, balanced meals, you've gained the tools to transform your dog's health and vitality. The journey you've embarked on doesn't end here; it evolves with each new meal you prepare, each tail wag, and every extra bounce in your dog's step.

We hope that the 30-day meal plan has set the foundation for your dog's transition to homemade food and that the secret ingredients for a shiny coat and fresh breath have brought noticeable changes. Continue to use the portion size formula to tailor each meal to your dog's changing dietary requirements as they age, grow, and change.

Sharing your life with a dog is a journey of unconditional love and companionship. Providing them with the best nutrition is not just an act of care—it's an expression of love. Keep this cookbook handy, revisit your favorite recipes, and continue to explore new ingredients and adjustments to suit your dog's tastes and health needs.

Thank you for trusting us to be a part of your dog's health and happiness. Here's to many more joyful years of companionship and culinary discovery together! Keep cooking, keep caring, and most importantly, keep loving your dog with every homemade meal.

🐾 Thank You for Choosing Our "Homemade Healthy Dog Food Cookbook"! 🐾

Hello there!
We're thrilled you've decided to explore the delightful world of homemade dog food with our cookbook. By now, you've probably whipped up a few tasty treats and meals, seeing firsthand those wagging tails and eager eyes at dinner time. Isn't knowing exactly what's going into your dog's bowl wonderful?

Your Thoughts Mean the World to Us!

We're on a mission to make healthy, homemade dog meals accessible to all, and your feedback is crucial in this journey. Whether it's a story about your dog's new favorite recipe, suggestions, or your overall experience with the book, we'd love to hear it!

Leave Us a Review on Amazon – It's Quick & Easy!

1. **Visit Amazon:**
   Go to Amazon.com and log in to your account.
2. **Find Our Cookbook:**
   Type "Homemade healthy dog food cookbook: 2 in 1 guide and cookbook with Simple, Fast, Nutritious, and Scrumptious Recipes. A balanced vet-approved diet to boost your pet's longevity and happiness".
3. **Write a Review:**
   Scroll down to the "Customer Reviews" section on the product page.
   Click on "Write a customer review."
   Share your thoughts and experiences with the book!

Every review helps us improve and informs fellow dog lovers about what they can expect from our "Homemade Healthy Dog Food Cookbook"
Thank you for being an amazing part of our community. Your support not only helps us grow, but it also helps us continue our commitment to happy, healthy dogs everywhere!
Warmest woofs and wags.

Made in the USA
Monee, IL
09 March 2025